SECOND EDITION

# SPLICING MODERN ROPES

## A PRACTICAL HANDBOOK

### JAN-WILLEM POLMAN

ADLARD
COLES

LONDON · OXFORD · NEW YORK · NEW DELHI · SYDNEY

ADLARD COLES
Bloomsbury Publishing Plc
50 Bedford Square, London, WC1B 3DP, UK

BLOOMSBURY, ADLARD COLES, and the buoy logo are trademarks of Bloomsbury Publishing Plc

First published in the Netherlands 2014 by Uitgeverij Hollandia BV
First published in English 2016
This edition published 2025

© 2020, 2025 Jan-Willem Polman

Originally published under the title *Handboek splitsen van modern lijnen* by Uitgeverij Hollandia BV,
Haarlem, The Netherlands; a division of Gottmer Uitgeversgroep BV

Jan-Willem Polman has asserted his right under the Copyright,
Designs and Patents Act, 1988, to be identified as Authors of this work

Photographs: Jan-Willem Polman, except p1 & p2 (© Gottifredi Maffioli Spa)
and p14 (© Spinlock)

Dyneema is a registered trademark of Avient Corporation

For legal purposes the Acknowledgements on p187 constitute an extension of
this copyright page

A catalogue record for this book is available from the British Library

Library of Congress Cataloguing-in-Publication data has been applied for

ISBN: HB: 978-1-3994-1726-6; ePub: 978-1-3994-1728-0; ePDF: 978-1-3994-1727-3

2 4 6 8 10 9 7 5 3 1

Typeset by Susan McIntyre
Printed and bound in India by Replika Press Pvt. Ltd.

MIX
Paper | Supporting
responsible forestry
FSC™ C016779

To find out more about our authors and books visit
www.bloomsbury.com and sign up for our newsletters

# Contents

## Brand names used

**Cordura** is a registered brand of Invista  **www.invista.com**

**Dacron** is a registered brand of Invista  **www.invista.com**

**Diolen** is a registered brand of FR Safety Yarns  **www.frsafety.de**

**D-Splicer** is a registered brand of D-Splicer B.V.  **www.d-splicer.com**

**Dyneema** is a registered brand of Avient Corporation  **www.Dyneema.com**

**Kevlar** is a registered brand of E. I. DuPont de Nemours and Company  **www.dupont.com**

**Selma** is a registered brand of Selma AS  **www.selma.no**

**Spectra** is a registered brand of Honeywell International Inc.  **www.honeywell-advancedfibers andcomposites.com**

**Technora** is a registered brand of Teijin Techno Products Ltd  **www.teijinaramid.com**

**Vectran** is a registered brand of Kuraray America Inc.  **www.vectranfiber.com**

**Zylon** is a registered brand of Toyobo Co Ltd.  **www.toyobo-global.com**

# Introduction

An eye splice in braided ropes is often left to a rigger or chandler or the rope is simply knotted. However, not only is splicing a fun thing to do, but most of the techniques are quite easy to learn.

The most important reason for learning how to splice is that you will get much more from your materials. A knot can reduce the tractive power of a rope by as much as 50%, whereas a well-spliced rope reduces strength by only around 5–10%.

You can also adapt your splicing to meet whatever needs you have on board, and splice a rope to make your setup easier, safer or faster.

If you're a competition sailor the techniques you'll learn in this book will optimise your deck layout and save weight on board. It's quite easy to replace much of the steel wire you carry on board with Dyneema, and techniques such as tapering a rope can save weight.

Why not splice an extra cover for a better grip in clutches or to extend the lifespan of your rope? There are all kinds of techniques in this book and you'll soon see that their uses are pretty much boundless.

The first part of this book describes various materials and how to use them on board. This insight will help you make a selection when buying new ropes. There is no real need to read these chapters first, but before you start splicing be sure to read the general instructions in Chapter 4. Otherwise, start anywhere and consult this book in any way you like.

# 1 Synthetic fibres

## Developments

In modern rope production, synthetic fibres have quickly come to replace natural fibres such as hemp and flax. These days it's rare to see anything on board other than synthetic ropes. It's no wonder, really, as synthetics have many advantages and have been developed very rapidly since the discovery that they could be produced from crude oil. In 1938 DuPont discovered nylon fibre, the first polyester was developed in 1941 and in early 1979 DSM applied for the patent for Dyneema.

It can be hard to make sense of the many chemical names for synthetic fibres (which are often indicated in the brand name), but it's well worth knowing something about the materials involved before you buy ropes. Polyester and polyamide belong to the first generation of synthetic fibres and are still used for making rope. The second generation, the so-called high-performance fibres, stem from these: LCP (Vectran) comes from polyester, and various aramid fibres (eg Kevlar, Twaron and Technora) are made from polyester or polyamide. The newest generation of fibres includes UHMWPE (Dyneema, Spectra) and PBO (Zylon).

## Materials by generation

| First generation conventional fibres | Second generation high-performance fibres | Third generation high-performance fibres |
|---|---|---|
| Polyolefins (PP & PE) | | HMPE or UHMWPE = Ultra High Molecular Weight Polyethylene Brand names: Dyneema, Spectra |
| Polyester (PET or PES) Brand names: Dacron, Diolen | LCP = Liquid Crystal Polymer Brand names: Vectran | |
| Polyamide (PA) Brand names: Nylon, Cordura | Aramid Brand names: Kevlar, Technora | PBO = Polybenzobisoxazole Brand name: Zylon |

*Note: only the most common brand names have been included here.*

There is still a great deal of work going on to further improve synthetic fibres. Every material has its advantages as well as its disadvantages, making each suitable for a variety of uses.

The most important differences are breaking load, wear, heat/UV resistance and stretch (see Appendix 1)

# Technical features

## Breaking load

The breaking load is the maximum direct force that a rope can take before it breaks. The breaking load of a rope is expressed in decanewton (daN)* or kilonewton (kN) or kilogram (kg). One manufacturer will have a greater safety margin in terms of breaking load than the other; which is why you should use these numbers only as an indication.

## Safe working load

The safe working load (SWL) of a rope is the recommended limit on the strain a rope is subjected to. Generally, around 20% of the breaking load is used as a safe working load. In practice, however, sails are usually reefed or the boat is in a safe harbour before a rope is loaded to its maximum.

## Stretch/Elongation

The stretch or elongation of a rope is often expressed as a percentage, measured to a particular load (for example, x percent of the breaking load). The more a rope is loaded, the more stretch it will have. When you're comparing stretch in ropes, make sure that the numbers relate to the same degree of load. Stretch properties are determined by a rope's material and construction; for example, the way it is braided affects stretch.

## Creep

Stretch in synthetic fibres also depends on how you load a rope: dynamically or statically. On running rigging (sheets, halyards, trim ropes, running backstays) the load is dynamic: a rope is tensioned and then released again. On standing rigging the load is static: once a stay has been tensioned, the same tension will be maintained for a long time.

'Creep' occurs when a rope slowly becomes longer; eventually the rope may break. After you've been out sailing, a halyard returns to the original length once pressure is released. But a long-lasting load on a rope can result in synthetic fibres not returning to their original length; this means a lasting stretch, or creep. Ropes that suffer from a lot of creep are not suitable for standing rigging. The degree of creep depends on temperature, load (per cent or breaking load) and time. Creep is greatest in warm climates where ropes are heavily loaded.

# Synthetic fibres used for ropes

## Polyester (PES)

You'll find polyester on the market under brand names such as Dacron and Diolen. Polyester ropes are relatively cheap to buy and usually have sufficient functionality for cruising sailors. They are often also used as covers around high-performance fibres.

The greatest disadvantage of polyester is the relatively high stretch – less than a rope made from polyamide and polypropylene, but more than newer fibres such as Dyneema. Polyester ropes don't float. They are resistant against sunlight and the strands are not affected by bacteria and mould.

Polyester fibres are available in various strength grades. The most commonly used ropes are made from high tenacity (HT) fibres, which are stronger than standard fibres.

*Newton is the unit used to express force: 1 daN = 1.0197 kilogram; 1 kN = 101.97 kilogram.*

Polyester staple (or spun) is another term used in the specification of ropes. Polyester filament fibres can be kilometres long, while polyester staple fibres are just centimetres long. These short fibres give a fuzzy, almost woolly effect. This material is used for covers on sheets.

## Polyamide (PA)

Polyamide is better known under its brand name Nylon. It is strong, supple, has quite a lot of stretch, sinks and is pretty UV resistant. It also absorbs water, which increases its stretch and decreases its strength. Its high stretch means that polyamide is suitable only for mooring lines. Cordura, another polyamide fibre, is often used in drysuits, to reinforce knees and seat, and for better grip in rope covers.

## Polypropylene (PP, PPM)

Polypropylene (also called polypropene or PP) is a synthetic fibre with moderate wear resistance and low durability. Polypropylene ropes are rough and therefore a 'pleasure' to hold. Polypropylene is so light that it floats, but it doesn't absorb water. It is not as strong as polyamide or polyester but can be manufactured much more inexpensively. Quality can vary quite significantly. The strength and price are lower if the polypropylene hasn't undergone UV treatment. Polypropylene is mainly used for mooring or towing lines but can also be used as lightweight fill in the core of ropes.

## UHMWPE/HMPE (Dyneema, Spectra)

Most people use the term HMPE (High Modulus Polyethylene) but the formal chemical term is UHMWPE (Ultra High Molecular Weight Polyethylene). However, the material is best known by the brand name Dyneema, so for that reason we will use Dyneema throughout the instructions when talking about splicing HMPE fibres. Dyneema was a brand of DSM that has been on the market since 1990. In September 2022 DSM sold the company to the Avient Corporation. Honeywell produces a similar fibre under the brand name Spectra. For many years both manufacturers were the only producers, due to patent restrictions, but in the last few years several alternative producers have come to the market. Some new producers make good HMPE quality yarns, but the special Dyneema grades like SK99 and DM20 are still quite unique.

Dyneema's extremely long molecules give it high strength and high wear resistance and it is so light that it floats. Generally speaking, Dyneema is a little bit stronger than steel of an equal diameter.

Be aware that Dyneema has a low melting point of only 145°C. At temperatures above 60°C strength decreases and elongation increases.

Dyneema doesn't absorb water and has the same characteristics whether wet or dry. It is also highly UV resistant and very smooth, which means that it doesn't grip well in cleats or in the hand.

In situations where you don't need a cover, you can easily remove the cover in order to save weight ('tapering'). This works well with spinnaker sheets, for example.

Dyneema fibres can be found in various versions, with the most common SK38, SK78 and SK99. The higher the number, the lower the stretch and stronger the fibre. Sailors will notice the difference in performance between SK38 and SK78 fibres. However, SK99 fibres are reserved mostly for off-shore racing. This is explained further in Appendix 1.

Dyneema will stretch under long-lasting static load (creep). This makes Dyneema less suitable for standing rigging, except for adjustable back-stays and runners. There is, however, a special Dyneema version called DM20 especially developed to be resistant against creep. Other versions of Dyneema are less sensitive for creep if the load is less than 10% of the breakload.

The difference in quality between Dyneema ropes is also determined by the quantity of Dyneema fibres in a rope. In the cheaper ropes, the Dyneema fibres in the core are mixed with other materials, for example polypropylene, and there may also be an extra inner cover made from polyester. By mixing it with other fibres the breakload will decrease and the stretch will increase.

## LCP (Vectran)

Liquid Crystal Polymer (LCP) is primarily known as Vectran. Vectran is similar to Dyneema but does not suffer from creep. The rope barely stretches and it's this feature that makes Vectran suitable for use as forestay or backstay. Its disadvantage is poor UV resistance. The fibre has to be protected from this by a cover at all times. Dyneema is often chosen over Vectran, primarily because it is lighter, harder wearing and more UV resistant.

## PBO (Zylon)

Polybenzobisoxazole (PBO) is often sold under the brand name Zylon. It has the least stretch of all the fibres, seriously high tractive power and no creep. Moreover, it has a very high temperature resistance.

PBO is, however, vulnerable to chemicals and its main disadvantage is its UV sensitivity. Without a cover, a PBO fibre that is exposed to UV for 24 hours will lose 50% of its breaking load. This is why PBO always has to have a cover; and you need to keep checking that the cover is not damaged.

PBO is used in synthetic rigging and in the cover of backstay runners in regattas such as the America's Cup. The force on these types of boats is so great that there is a risk of juddering when they're flexing under tension. However, PBO ropes are easily damaged and therefore have to be replaced often – something that can be too costly for most sailors, given that PBO isn't exactly the cheapest of fibres.

## Aramid (Kevlar, Technora)

Aramid fibres are often sold under the brand names Kevlar and Technora. Aramid is a strong fibre with very little stretch and good resistance to high temperatures (aramid fibres retain their strength and shape up to around 270°C, Dyneema fibres only to 70°C). It also doesn't suffer from creep. However, if it is used under a small block at a tight angle, it will get damaged.

Until the 1990s there were many ropes with an aramid core, but it has since lost ground to Dyneema, which is lighter and more resistant against bending fatigue. Because of its high heat resistance, aramid is now mainly used for covers. On racing boats the friction on a winch can become so great that a polyester cover will melt. In this kind of situation, aramid is often used in the cover.

# 2 Construction of ropes

The construction of a rope largely determines how you must splice it. Ropes are either twisted or braided. As well as this, they either have a core or do not. Moreover, the core can also be constructed in a variety of ways.

## Classic plaited or twisted ropes

A twisted rope consists of a number of strands twisted together. Twisted ropes are mainly used for mooring and anchor lines and on classic ships for other purposes too. For thicker diameters one often chooses eight-strand or twelve-strand ropes. These are actually braided ropes.

**Three-strand rope:** Made from three strands twisted around each other.
- To learn how to make an eye splice in three-strand rope, go to page 22.

**Eight-strand rope:** Made from two pairs of right-twisted and two pairs of left-twisted strands. The right-twisted strands are sometimes marked with a control line.
- To learn how to make an eye splice in eight-strand rope, go to page 25.
- To learn more about splicing this rope to anchor chain, go to page 30.

**Twelve-strand rope:** Made from six right-twisted and six left-twisted strands.
- To learn how to make an eye splice in twelve-strand rope, go to page 34.

# Single braid ropes

A single braid rope is made up of an even number of strands. The most common is the 12-strand single braid Dyneema rope. Depending on how tightly it is braided, this can be easily spliced and used for a variety of purposes on board. A polyester lanyard is also a single braid rope.

A second type of single braid rope consists of only a high grip cover. This kind is mainly used on open boats as a (light weather) sheet.

**A single braid rope consisting of a braided core:**
- To learn how to make eye splices in single braid Dyneema, go to page 56.
- To learn how to make soft shackles of Dyneema, go to page 92.
- To learn how to join two single braid Dyneema ropes, go to page 112.
- To learn how to join single braid Dyneema and double braid polyester, go to page 121.
- To learn how to make a continuous loop of single braid Dyneema, go to page 150.
- To learn how to make soft fids, go to page 177.

**A single braid rope** consisting of a braided cover containing a grip fibre. This is also **sometimes called a hollow braid** and is used as a sheet on open boats.
- To learn how to make eye splices in single braid Dyneema, go to page 59.
- To learn how to join two single braid Dyneema ropes, go to page 112.

# Double braid ropes

A double braid rope has both a braided cover and a braided core. The cover is often made of polyester, with the core varying in terms of material. The more space there is between the core and the cover, the easier it is to splice these ropes. Some ropes have an inner cover between the core and cover; this mostly serves as filling.

A double braid rope with a polyester core: the cover is spliced in for strength.

- To learn how to make eye splices in double braid polyester rope, go to page 38.
- To learn how to join double braid polyester to steel wire, go to page 115.
- To learn how to join single braid Dyneema to double braid polyester, go to page 121.
- To learn how to make a continuous loop in double braid polyester, go to page 138.

A double braid rope with a core of high-performance fibres (such as Dyneema): the cover doesn't have to be spliced in for strength but possibly for UV resistance (for example, in Vectran ropes).

- To learn how to make eye splices in double braid Dyneema, go to page 72.
- To learn how to taper double braid Dyneema, go to page 110.
- To learn how to make a continuous loop from double braid Dyneema, go to page 159.

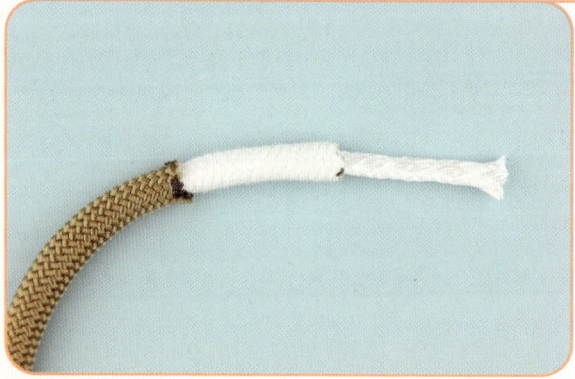

A double braid rope with an inner cover and core of high-performance fibres (such as Dyneema).

- To learn how to make eye splices in double braid Dyneema with an inner cover, go to page 84.

# Braided cover with a core of twisted strands or parallel fibre

Rather than having a braided core, polyester ropes can also come with a core made from twisted strands or parallel fibres. These ropes have relatively less stretch than double braid polyester ones. The fibres in the core are more in line with the direction of the load on the rope and a core with parallel fibres does not suffer from braid stretch. These ropes are more difficult to splice than double braid ropes.

**A line with a core of twisted strands:**
- To learn how to make eye splices in a polyester rope with a twisted core, go to page 44.

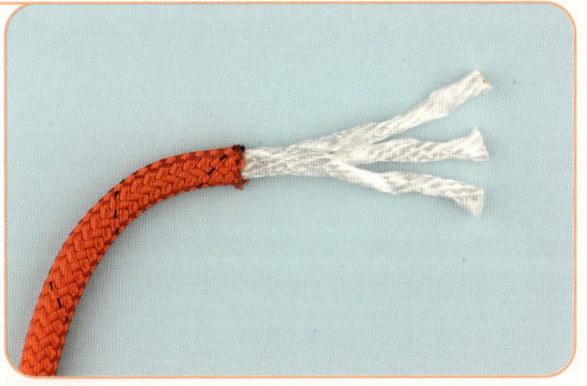

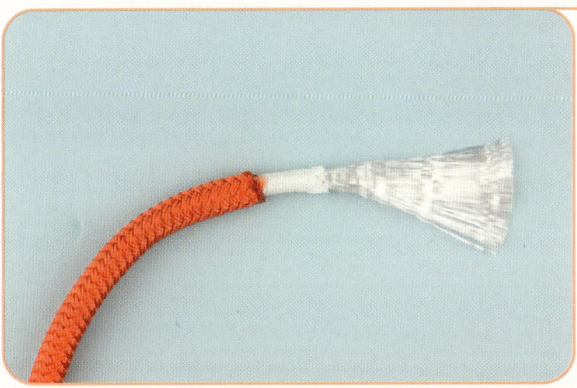

**A line with a core of parallel fibres:**
- To learn how to make eye splices in a polyester rope with a core of parallel fibres, go to page 51.

# Additional types of rope construction

A rope's characteristics are largely determined by the fibres used and the construction, but manufacturers also apply a number of additional treatments.

Dyneema fibres are often treated with a coating to make them stay in place better. This also makes them easier to work with. Because Dyneema fibres are so smooth, you'd need to push uncoated Dyneema much further back into itself to achieve a decent strength when making an eye splice.

A number of manufacturers sell pre-stretched ropes, which have had the braid stretch – or construction stretch – (i.e. the stretch that still remains after the production process) removed. This significantly decreases the rope's overall stretch. Once you've been using a rope for a while that hasn't been pre-stretched, you'll get the same effect. Pre-stretching (usually with Dyneema) often happens at high temperatures. As a result, the fibres are compressed and better oriented in the direction of pull, which makes the line stronger and reduces stretch. These pre-stretched ropes are a bit stiffer.

There are also special anti-torsion ropes, which are used in furling systems. Their construction ensures equal pull along the full length of the luff.

# 3 Which type of rope?

Imagine you are in a chandler's staring at dozens of rolls of rope. How do you decide which rope you need? Unfortunately not even the salespeople always know the pros and cons of synthetic fibres, and their advice may be skewed by their commercial interests. With the information in this chapter, you should be able to choose the best materials for your sheets, halyards, control lines and mooring lines.

## Material for sheets and halyards

The most common combinations of fibres for cruising and racing yachts are given in the table below.

Popular material choices

| | Cruisers | | Performance cruisers | | Competition sailors | |
|---|---|---|---|---|---|---|
| | Core | Cover | Core | Cover | Core | Cover |
| **Halyards** | Polyester | Polyester | Dyneema SK38, Dyneema SK78 mix with other fibre or other HMPE | Polyester | 100% Dyneema SK78/ SK99 or other high quality HMPE | Polyester |
| **Sheets** | Polyester | Polyester with grip | Polyester | Polyester with grip | 100% Dyneema SK78/ SK99 or other high quality HMPE | Polyester with grip or Polyester mixed with an aramid |

*Professional competition sailors also use other fibres, such as PBO, Vectran and aramids like Kevlar and Technora (see Chapter 1).*

### Material for sheets

Two things are important for sheets: not too much stretch and a good grip. To be able to flatten your sail as much as possible, you need a sheet that doesn't stretch. If your mainsheet runs through multiple blocks, the force on the rope is reduced to the point that you won't need to worry about stretch.

Grip is not as important on boats over 11.5 metres (38ft), because the sheets are thick enough to have good grip and are used only with a winch. In this case, you can use the same cover as on your halyards.

Good grip can be achieved in various ways; the most economical method is a cover of polyester staple (see page 4). Ropes with covers of mixed fibres (Cordura, Vectran or aramids mixed with polyester) are more expensive. Aramid fibres are applied not only to improve grip, but also to protect against heat build-up on a winch.

Lightweight sheets are important for rounded sails such as spinnakers; they will produce a nicely rounded sail even in light weather. You can make your sheets lighter by 'tapering' them (see page 110); ready-made tapered sheets are also available. Tapering only makes sense for ropes with a Dyneema core. Since the Dyneema core provides the strength of the rope and the cover does not contribute, you do not need the cover. For polyester ropes both the core and cover contribute to the strength of the rope, so you cannot take the cover away without compromising the rope.

## Material for halyards

Halyards should have as little stretch as possible. Always choose a rope with a full Dyneema SK78 or SK99 (or other high quality HMPE) core for laminate sails. Most cruisers sail with Dacron sailcloth and have the choice of ropes with a polyester or Dyneema core, depending on their budget. In the past few years there has been a clear trend for cruisers to switch to Dyneema for their halyards.

For performance cruisers there are a few more affordable options. As a compromise, you could have a hybrid core, with Dyneema SK78 fibres mixed with another fibre. This can be either by using an inner cover (often from polyester staple) or by braiding the core from a mix of Dyneema SK78 with another fibre (often PP). Another possibility is using cheaper Dyneema SK38. A third option is not to use Dyneema but a competitor's HMPE. A full core from good quality HMPE is often similar in price to the hybrid Dyneema core options, but with a much better performance (see Appendix 1).

For cruising yachts a spinnaker or gennaker halyard is allowed to stretch. These rounded sails must bear gusts of wind; if the halyard doesn't stretch the sail takes the full force. However, if you are reaching with your spinnaker, which racing yachts are often doing, a Dyneema halyard is recommended.

A code zero halyard always requires a full Dyneema SK78 or SK99 (or other high quality HMPE) core. The halyard is tightening the code zero rope, which works as a forestay. Often these halyards even have a 1:2 purchase in order to apply sufficient tension.

For the spinnaker halyard on a dinghy, it is useful to have grip fibre in the cover, as described for sheets above. Just like the sheets, a spinnaker halyard is continuously handled during a race.

## Material for control lines and running backstays

Again, you need as little stretch as possible in control lines such as boom vang, Cunningham, outhaul and traveller to be able to get the sail as flat as possible.

Choose Dyneema lines if you are a competition sailor. You should use a Dyneema core, especially if you're using a line without a purchase system.

On cruising boats where the control lines run through blocks, polyester cores can be used.

Depending on the application you can also choose to have grip fibres in the cover, as described for sheets above.

## Diameter and breaking load for sheets and halyards

The diameter of sheets and halyards has to fit in with the clutches, cleats and blocks on board. It is recommended to choose a rope that is 1–2mm thinner than the maximum diameter of a block.

Some boats have a steel lead on their halyard. How to splice a steel lead or single braid Dyneema to a polyester halyard is explained in Chapter 9.

If you're planning to replace your halyards and sheets with a polyester core with Dyneema you could use thinner lines because Dyneema is about three times stronger than polyester. Usually 2mm is taken off the diameter for Dyneema ropes. Be aware that the holding power of your clutch decreases if you go down in rope diameter.

The following equations can be used to calculate the breaking load needed for your sheets and halyards. The resulting values compare with the numbers used by rope manufacturers (in kg or daN, with 1daN = 10,197kg). A safety factor of 5 is used in the equations, which means that a rope will receive a workload of only 20% of the breaking load (see also page 3). For example, if you have a mainsail with an area of 25m2, the mainsheet (without blocks) and the mainsail halyard need to have a breaking load of 2,500kg (2,550daN)).

|  | Breaking loads sheets (kg) | Breaking loads halyards (kg) |
|---|---|---|
| **Headsail** | Sail area (m²) × 80 | Sail area (m²) × 80 |
| **Mainsail** | Sail area (m²) × 100* | Sail area (m²) × 100 |
| **Spinnaker/gennaker** | Sail area (m²) × 30* | Sail area (m²) × 30 |

*Source: Cousin Trestec*

*Note: A mainsheet is always used in a purchase system so it can be thinner for breaking load. To calculate the breaking load of the mainsheet you can divide the formula by the purchase.*

If you want to be more precise in calculating the workload on your sheets and halyards, you can use the Marshall Formula as explained in Appendix 2.

In Appendix 2 you can also find a table listing the correct diameters of sheets and halyards. For these calculations it is assumed that the ropes will be spliced. If you're using a knot instead, figure in a 50% loss of strength.

## Length for sheets and halyards

Your type of boat and sail plan are the most important factors in determining the length of your ropes. The best way to figure out what length you need is to measure your old ropes when you want to replace them. Most manufacturers use the following guidelines:

**Length guidelines**

|  | Length of sheets (m) | Length of halyards (m) |
|---|---|---|
| **Headsail** | Boat length × 1.5 | Mast height × 2.5 |
| **Mainsail** | Boom length × 5 for 4:1 purchase<br>Boom length × 7 for 6:1 purchase<br><br>General:<br>Boom length × (purchase+1) | Mast height × 2.5 |
| **Spinnaker** | Boat length × 2 | Mast height × 2.5 |

# Mooring lines

Mooring lines need to be able to absorb the shocks caused by wind and water to protect the deck hardware they're attached to. That's why mooring lines need stretch. The cheapest ones are made of polypropylene (PPM). They also float, which is useful for tow lines. However, polypropylene is not very UV resistant or durable, and it can crack.

The most durable option would be a polyester or polyamide mooring line. Please note that a polyester mooring line could still have a polypropylene core. If you can hear it crack while rolling it through your fingers, you are dealing with polypropylene.

Mooring lines are available in laid and double braid constructions. The choice between these depends on your personal preference. Laid ropes have a little more stretch than double braid ropes, but they are more susceptible to wear by friction compared with other ropes.

When one strand is worn through, the whole construction is gone and you need to replace the rope (according to Samson Rope, you need to replace a laid rope when it has 10% damage and a braid rope only when it has 50% damage). A braid rope is more flexible, less noisy and has a better feel.

## Diameter for mooring lines

The following rule of thumb is often used to determine the diameter of mooring lines: take the boat length in metres and add 2 – this is the diameter you need in millimetres. So, on a 10-metre boat you need mooring lines of 12mm. Since polypropylene ropes are weaker you'll need a thicker rope if you're using this fibre. In Appendix 2 you'll find the guidelines for the diameter of mooring lines in relation to boat length and weight.

## Length for mooring lines

For mooring lines you usually take one to one-and-a-half times the boat length. Again, this also depends on your personal preference. Usually you'd have at least two mooring lines one-and-a-half times the boat length and two mooring lines of one boat length on board. An anchor rode is commonly five times the maximum water depth.

It is useful to splice a bespoke mooring line if you have a fixed mooring. You can protect this line with a cover or a stainless steel thimble at critical points.

# Ropes combined with clutches

A rope and a clutch form a critical combination. Make sure you have the right clutch size for your ropes. A clutch has the most holding strength at the specified maximum diameter. Decreasing rope diameter by 2mm roughly reduces the holding power by 20%. The part that jams to hold the rope, called the cam, can sometimes be replaced with a smaller or larger one.

If you have a rope that is too thin for your clutch or a clutch that is too light for the application, the line may slip, which causes it severe wear. A new halyard could be worn through in one day.

If a cam is worn out a little it can cause the rope to slip and may work like a knife on the rope. You therefore need to check your cams annually and replace them when necessary. You could also splice an extra cover or core into your rope to thicken it where needed (see Chapter 10).

Releasing a clutch in one go can damage a rope's cover. It is therefore always better to hold the rope on a winch before you take the tension off the clutch. This lengthens the life expectancy of both clutch and rope.

Bear in mind that you will get more tension on the clutches if you replace polyester halyards with Dyneema. Polyester takes some of the force of wind gusts because it has more stretch.

With Dyneema ropes, all the force is transferred to the clutch. That's why there are specialised Dyneema rope clutches. They are bigger and stronger, and have a larger cam surface area to hold the rope.

# Maintenance and troubleshooting

Your life could depend on certain ropes, so you need to inspect them regularly. Never step on a rope and avoid sand and chemicals because they can damage the fibres.

### Inspection

Check for differences in thickness. This indicates broken strands in the core. Colouring can be caused by a chemical reaction with the fibres. Polyester fibres, for example, are less resistant to certain types of alkaline (soap).

Wear in the cover means a direct loss of breaking load for ropes with a polyester core, because the strength in these ropes is provided by both the core and the cover. Ropes with a Dyneema core get all their strength from the core; a worn-out cover is therefore less critical.

When you start to use single braid Dyneema ropes, the outside gets fuzzy quickly, because the filaments break and that serves as a protective layer for the fibres underneath. If you open up the strands and you see crushed and broken fibres, it means that there has been some wear.

A general rule is to replace single braid ropes at 25% wear (or when you see broken fibres).

Double braid polyester ropes have to be replaced at 50% wear of the cover and three-strand laid ropes at 10% wear.

If you see a strand looping out from a rope without it being cut, it will not have an effect on the breaking load; you can just tuck it back in.

## Friction and wear

Regularly check for screws or other protruding objects that ropes can catch on. Use fairleads to lead lines. Splicing in a stainless steel thimble (see Chapter 6), a protective cover (see Chapter 5) or an extra Dyneema cover (see Chapter 10) can lengthen the life expectancy of a rope.

I once had a gennaker come down while I was in the middle of the ocean, because a block on the mast had been continuously chafing the halyard. Inspect your blocks to check that the ropes are running through smoothly and are not worn.

If you are sailing in the tropics, UV radiation becomes more important in terms of rope wear.

From my own experience I know that, for example, polypropylene lifeline netting will break down within months. Choose polyester in sunny climates, especially for mooring lines.

## Rope does not hold in clutches

The wrong combination of clutch and rope will quickly wear out your ropes. This is easily avoided – see page 14.

## Twisted ropes

Ropes can deform if they're stowed under tension. You therefore have to make sure that all the kinks and twists are taken out before use. Knots have to be removed after use. A double braid rope always needs to be coiled with one hand so that it can be hung up in 'eights'. Ropes that twist under tension often have a core of laid strands.

## Cleaning ropes

Increase the durability of your ropes by taking them off the boat at the end of the season. Soak them in fresh water or tuck them into a tied pillowcase in the washing machine. If you want to use detergent, make sure it is mild and neutral. Washing the ropes will remove all the salt, sand and dirt. This allows the fibres to be aligned without friction so that the rope will be soft and efficient. After washing the rope you will have to air dry it.

# 4 Before you start

A knot can reduce the breaking load of a rope by half, while a splice reduces it by only 5–10%. It is useful if you can splice your own ropes because it is the weakest link that counts. The key to splicing in a braided rope is taking it far enough back into itself; this causes friction and the rope tightens itself. Splicing will work only in new ropes since the fibres will still be flexible.

## Splicing tools

Depending on the type of splice and rope, there is a variety of splicing tools available, such as Selma fids, D-Splicer pulling needles and traditional splicing fids. You'll probably also need a hot knife, scissors (both normal ones and ones specifically for Dyneema), tape, a marker pen, measuring tape, a needle, whipping twine, a knife and a cutting board.

Make sure you have enough space to work and an anchoring point for your rope. If you're on board you can use a winch in case you need extra force.

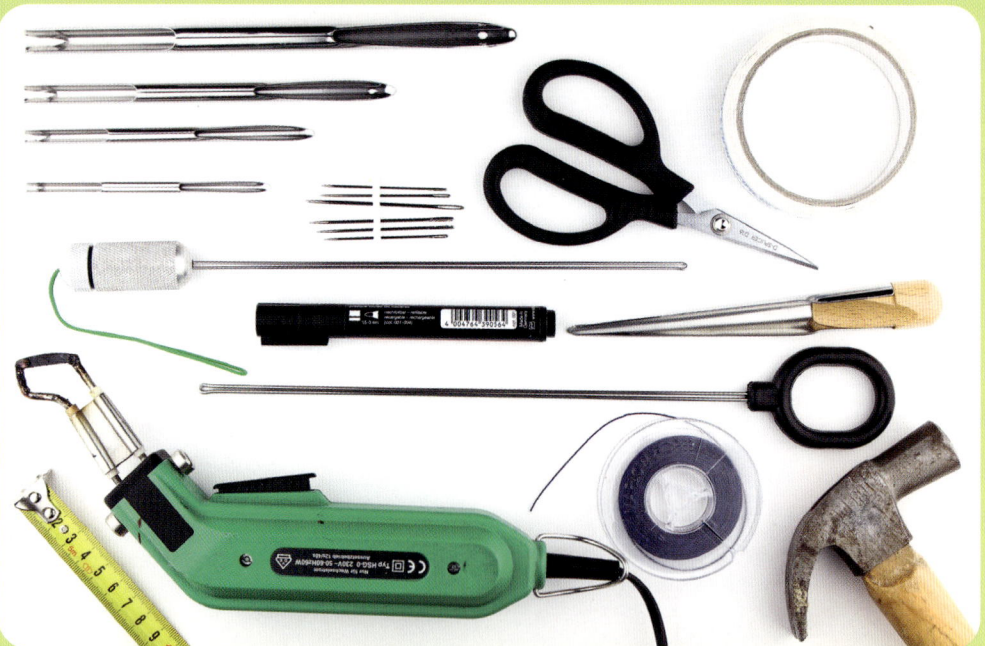

Use splicing tape to keep the ends of a rope together. You could also tape the end of the rope to the fid. There are various brands of specialised smooth, thin and strong splicing tape.

Choose a fid that matches the diameter of the rope, or even one that is slightly thinner.

Always use the same fid to measure distances to make sure the ratios are correct.

Make sure the smooth side of the fid is the one sliding along the rope. The other side has an indentation with which you might accidentally pull out some fibre – especially if you need to pass along another core into the cover. The same can happen with the point of the fid.

Use a soft fid (see Chapter 14) or a pulling needle in case the rope is too tight to slide a fid in. These are thinner and you can apply more force.

Never use pliers to pull out a fid from the rope – you will damage it!

# Splicing technique and core materials

There are two splicing methods for double braid ropes: one in which you need the cover of the rope to strengthen the eye splice (for ropes with polyester and polyamide cores), and another where you don't (for example in high-performance fibre ropes). It's very important to understand why this distinction is made.

The core provides almost the full strength of a rope with a high-performance fibre core such as Dyneema. You therefore don't need the cover in the splice to provide strength. You will need the cover to splice ropes with polyester (or polyamide) cores because the cover contributes about one third of the breaking load.

If you have a core made of high-performance fibres, you don't need the cover to strengthen the eye splice, but in some fibres (such as Vectran) it is needed for UV protection. Dyneema is very UV resistant so it can always be used without the cover.

### The size of the eye

Make sure the 'neck' of an eye splice is no wider than 30 degrees when there is a workload on it. (There are even stricter requirements for high performance fibre ropes such as Dyneema, where an eye splice should not be wider than 15 degrees and the length of the eye should therefore be at least five times the diameter of the object around which it goes.)

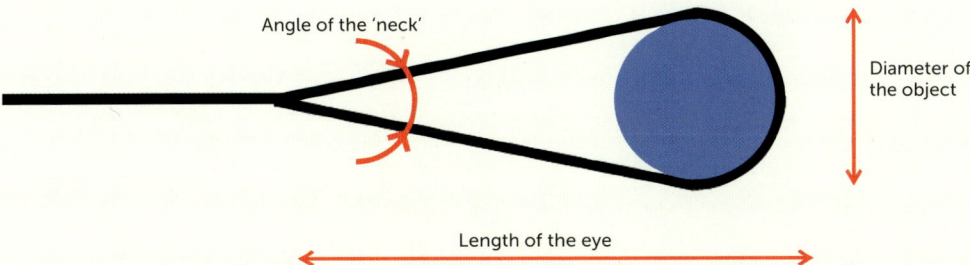

As a rule of thumb, the length of the eye should be at least 2.7 times the diameter of the object. This is less critical for halyards with a stainless steel lock. For example, if you're using a shackle with a diameter of 5mm, you need the spliced eye to be at least 1.3cm in length.

However, the rule is important for mooring lines that are used over a cleat. If your cleats on board have a diameter of 9cm, every mooring line eye needs to be at least 24cm long.

# How to remove core from the cover

Removing the core from the cover requires some practice. It is often easy to use a traditional splicing fid for this. With tightly braided ropes it takes a little more time than with looser braided ropes. Make sure that you do not accidentally pull a strand from the cover at step 3 below.

Pull the strands aside with a thin or hollow fid until you see the core.

Take the core out of the cover.

Pull the core further out.

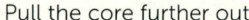

# 'Tapering' the ends of a rope

If the differences in diameter in a splice are large, you get localised tension, which weakens the rope, especially high-performance fibre ropes such as Dyneema. You should therefore try to achieve a gradual decrease in thickness of the rope you tuck in. This is done by cutting one end diagonally along the final third of the splice length, as shown in the images below.

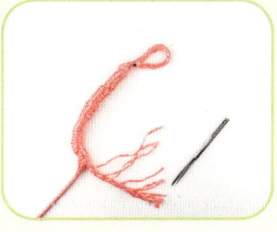 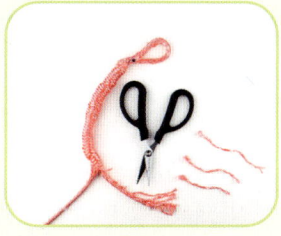 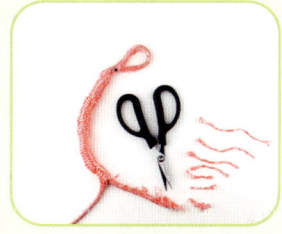

If you want to taper the end while losing less of the construction – to prevent loss of strength – you can slim a core or cover down more systematically. This usually happens when you splice two ropes together, like in the method for making continuous loops. After slimming the rope you can still splice it because the structure is preserved.

Here, the strands on both ends have been thinned by half, from the second mark on. The structure is preserved and the rope can still be spliced.

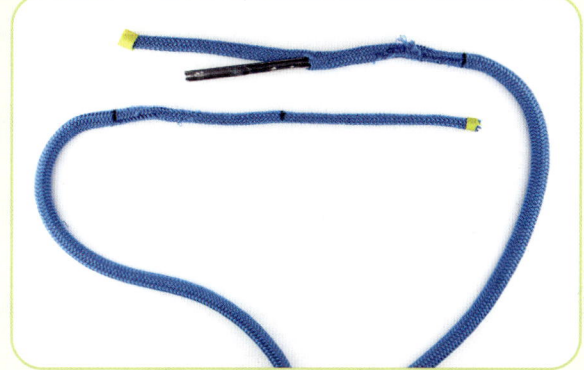

The next example is a 16-strand braided cover with eight pairs of strands braided to the left and eight pairs braided to the right.

Tape the end of the cover and cut off a short piece. Remove one strand of each pair.

Pull the strands out from the cover with a splicing fid and cut them.

The structure is preserved, but the rope is slimmed down with fewer strands.

## 'Milking' the cover

Sliding back the cover is also called 'milking'. Sometimes the last bit can be difficult. Attach the rope about two metres from the eye to an eye or cleat, and slide the cover back through your fist while you pull the loop back. For the final step, add some more tension on the rope and/or use a hammer.

Slide the cover towards the eye.

Add tension with a winch or use your weight (I often wear a climbing harness and attach it to the rope) if the milking is difficult.

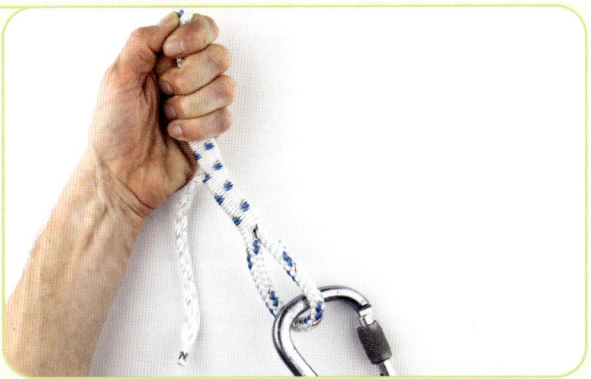

Use a hammer if the last bit is too hard. This loosens the fibres, which will allow you to slide the cover slightly further. Repeat this until the eye is finished.

## Long bury splice

If a rope has to disappear into itself or into another rope, make sure you have enough room. The rule of thumb is to take about one third extra length: if the rope to be hidden is 20cm long, you have to let it come out at 26cm. The rope into which the fid is inserted will ride up. Once the rope has gone through, taper it by cutting it diagonally. Slide back the cover and the buried rope disappears.

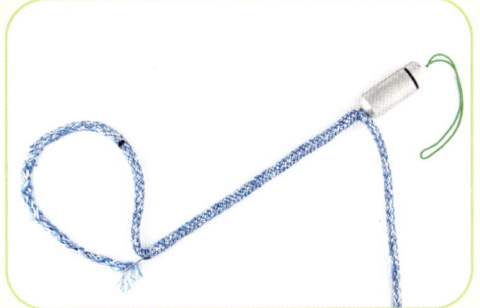

# 5 Splice in plaited or twisted ropes

## Three-strand rope

Most sailors can make an eye splice in a laid rope. Although this is a fairly traditional way of splicing, it is covered here for completeness. On modern yachts the techniques are still often used for splicing fender lines or mooring lines. The start is the most complicated part. Once you have all three strands tucked back into the rope correctly, it is only a matter of braiding.

Wrap some tape around the rope, about 25–35 cm in from its end (depending on the thickness of the rope).

1

Unlay the strands with a knife.

2

Determine the size of the eye and insert the fid at that point, at right angles to the direction of the lay.

3

4

Feed the middle loose strand below the lifted strand.

Twist the rope in the direction of the lay and feed through the next strand.

5

6

Two strands are now through; the white one is still loose.

Twist the rope back until you find the last strand under which nothing has been fed yet. Feed the last strand underneath.

All strands have been fed through once; now you can braid them.

Lead each strand over the adjacent strand and underneath the next one.

Braid all the strands at least three times through the rope. For industrial applications five times is often the standard.

For a tapered finish, braid the white strand once more and the blue one twice more. Then remove the tape and cut the ends.

11

This creates an eye splice in a three-strand rope.

12

# Eight-strand rope

An eight-strand rope consists of two left-twisting and two right-twisting pairs. Make sure the left-twisting strands are fed below left-twisting strands, and right-twisting strands below the right-twisting ones. Work systematically with different tape colours to prevent yourself from getting lost in the mess of strands. An eight-strand square plaited rope can be used as a mooring line or anchor rode.

Wrap some tape around the rope, about 25–35 cm in from the end (depending on the thickness of the rope).

Unlay the strands into four pairs and mark the left-twisting and right-twisting pairs with tape. Insert a fid into the rope, at right angles, under one pair of strands.

Pull through a right-twisting pair of strands under another right-twisting pair.

Then, in the opposite direction, pull through a left-twisting pair under a left-twisting pair.

Flip the line and repeat the previous steps for the remaining two pairs of strands.

Loosen the strands in one pair and braid them individually. These individual strands need to go underneath a single strand.

Repeat this at least three times and then tie a knot in the two strands.

Braid the other pairs, also at least three times per strand, and finish each pair with a knot.

The splice is now ready; for a nice tapered finish continue to braid one strand of each pair. Braid this strand underneath two strands rather than underneath one as before.

Repeat these steps with the next pairs to create a tapered end.

Melt or cut the eight strands.

This creates an eye splice in an eight-strand rope.

If you want to make your mooring lines more durable, splice a protective cover in the eye. Slide it over the line before you start splicing and sew it to the line with a few stitches.

# Eight-strand rope spliced to anchor chain

Anchor chain runs over a chain gypsy. The anchor chain can be spliced to an eight-strand rope. The transition from chain to rope will run smoothly over your gipsy when you use this splice technique. The eight-strand rope usually clamps well on the chain gypsy.

Make a mark on the 12th link of the chain. Wrap tape around the line at a distance of 12 links plus about 20cm from the end.

Unlay the strands into four pairs.

Insert two pairs with same twist direction (both left or both right) crosswise through the first link.

Now loosen the strands in one pair and put one strand of a pair through the third link.

From both pairs take one strand and braid it crosswise through the links (3rd, 5th, 7th, 9th, 11th, 13th) beyond the mark on the chain.

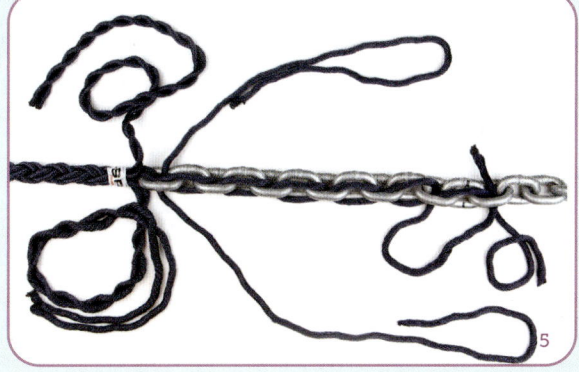

For the remaining strands do the same, but now the strand goes *below* the link.

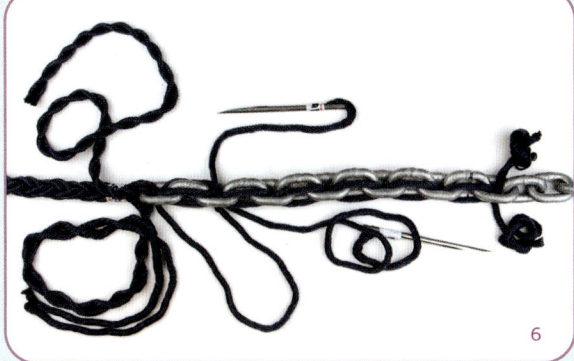

Turn the chain ninety degrees. Loosen the remaining two pairs and braid them through the chain in the same way only now through the 2nd, 4th, 6th, 8th, 10th and 12th, 14th and 16th links.

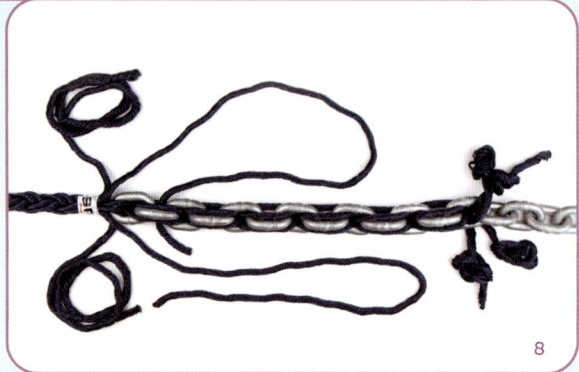

From both pairs, braid one strand *above* the links along.

And braid from both pairs one strand *below* the links along.

Take two strands coming from opposite directions from a link and connect them with a stitched whipping (page 164). Melt off the excess length.

Do the same for the other strands.

Remove the tape and make a stitched whipping.

This creates a connection between an eight-strand rope and an anchor chain.

# Twelve-strand rope

A twelve-strand rope consists of six left and six right twisted strands. For the best results, you first distribute the twelve strands evenly along the rope (steps 1 through 4) and then braid the individual strands through the line. This technique is used for thick mooring lines made of polypropylene or polyester, for example. Thicker single braided Dyneema lines from about 18mm and up are often spliced the same way. But in steps 5 through 8, you then braid the individual strands at least eight times under one strand.

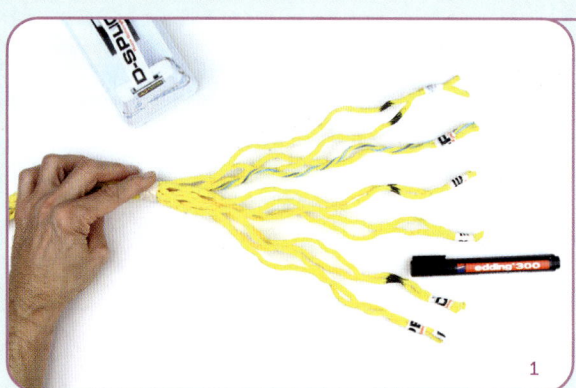

Wrap some tape around the rope, about 25–35cm in from the end (depending on the thickness of the rope). Unravel the strands and mark the left twisted strands. Make pairs of left and pairs of right twisted strands.

1

Insert a fid into the line under four strands. Braid a left and a right-handed pair through the line.

2

Insert the fid from the same point in opposite directions into the line again under four strands. Braid a left and a right-handed pair through the line.

You now have three bundles of two pairs evenly spaced along the line. For each bundle, you are now going to braid the strands through the line.

In the following steps, right-turned strands (red) alternately pass under a right-turned strand (red). Each strand passes under a strand *at least four times*.

The same goes for the left-turned strands (blue).

The first right-turned strand passes under a right-turned strand.

The second right-turned strand passes under a right-turned strand. Repeat steps 6 and 7 at least three more times.

In total, both strands pass under at least four strands each.

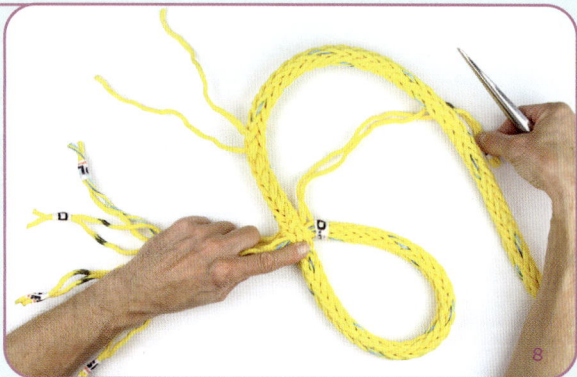

For a nicely tapered finish continue to braid one strand underneath two strands. Repeat one more time so that this strand passes under four strands in total.

Repeat steps 6 through 9 for the left-turned strands passing under a left-turned strand.

You now have one of the three bundles ready.

Repeat steps 6 to 11 for the other two bundles.

Melt off the ends. Often I let these stick out about 2cm.

This creates an eye splice in a twelve-strand rope.

# 6 Eye splice in polyester ropes

In ropes with a polyester core you need to use both the core and the cover for strength. There are three types of polyester core: braided, laid and parallel fibres.

Use a fid similar or slightly thinner than the diameter of the rope. Always use the same fid for measuring distances while splicing.

## Double braid rope

The method to splice a rope with a braided polyester core and polyester braided cover is explained below. This eye splice is well suited to having a shackle spliced in – skip step 7A if you don't want to do this.

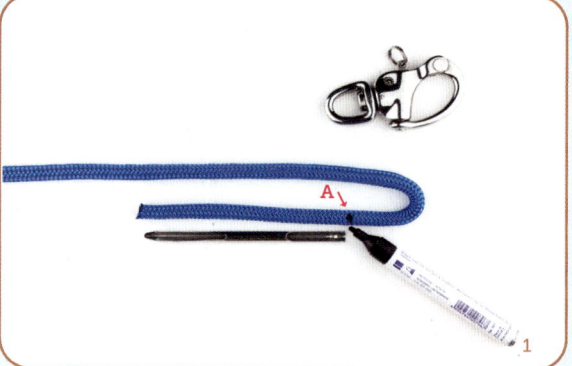

Cut a small piece of the rope to separate the cover from the core. Mark point A with a pen at one fid length from the end.

Determine the size of the eye and mark point B opposite point A.

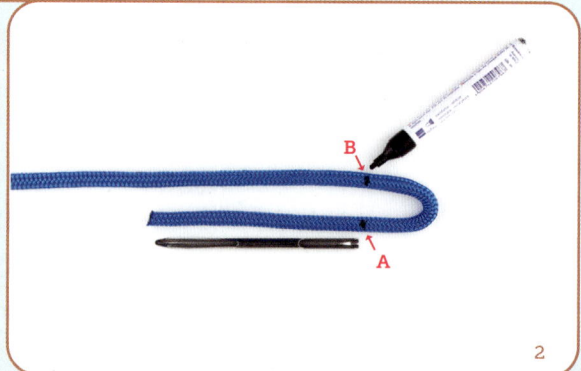

Take the core from the cover at
point B with a fid.

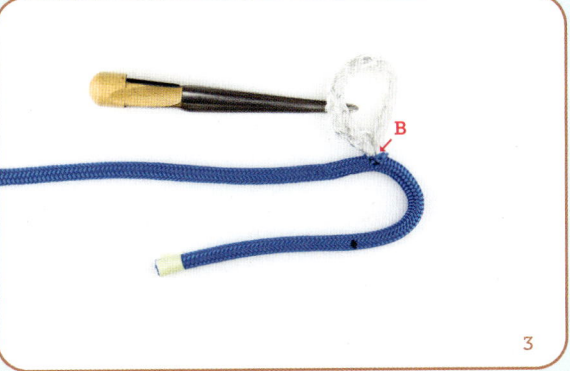

3

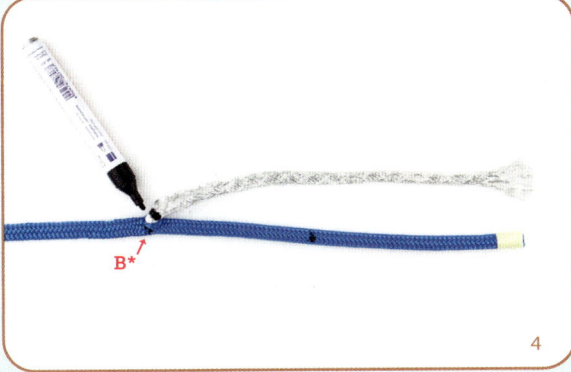

4

Mark the core at the point where it
comes out of the cover; this is
point B*.

Pull more core from the cover at B.
Wrap some tape around the core
and cover to prevent them from
coming apart.

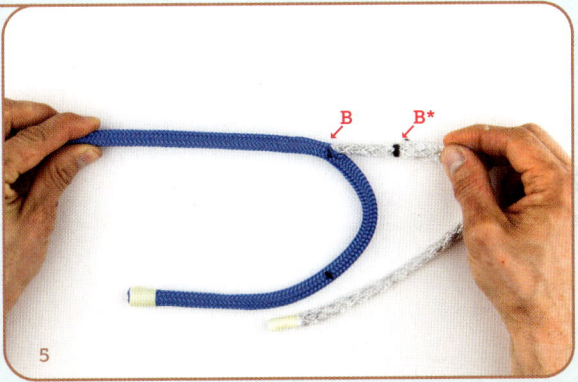

5

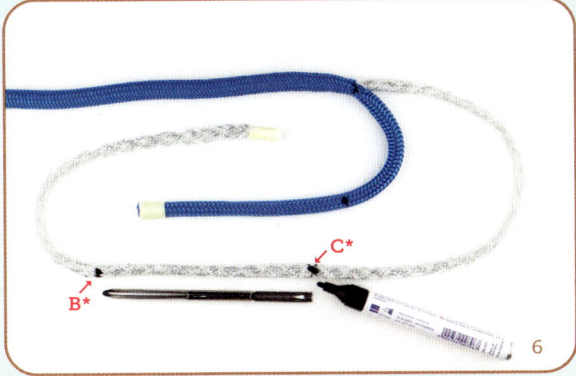

6

Mark point C* at one fid length
from point B* going away from the
end of the rope.

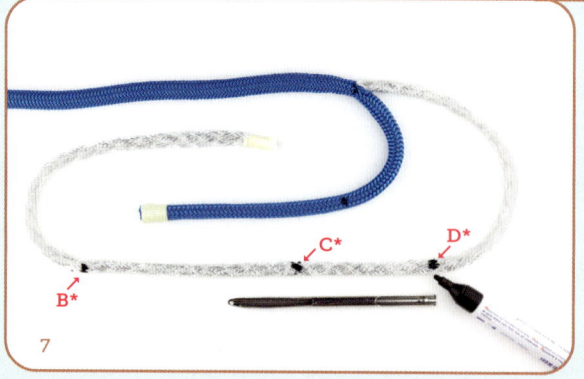

Mark point D* at three quarters of a fid length from point C*.

If you want to splice a shackle directly to the rope, you have to insert it around the cover now.

Insert a suitable fid into the core from C* to D* to pull through the cover.

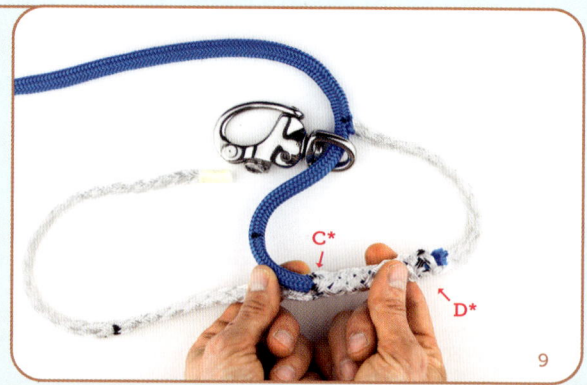

Remove the tape from the cover and cut it diagonally. Take the cover back into the core so that it disappears completely.

Insert a thin fid through the cover and core to prevent them from sliding.

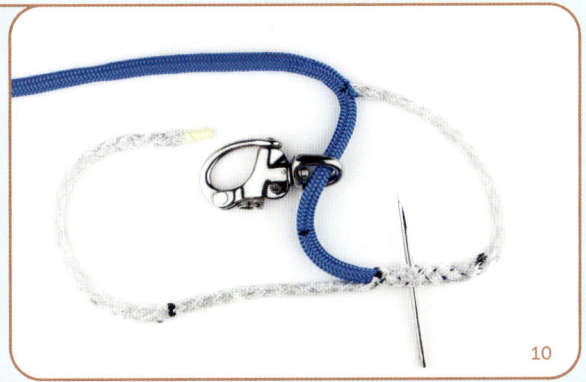

10

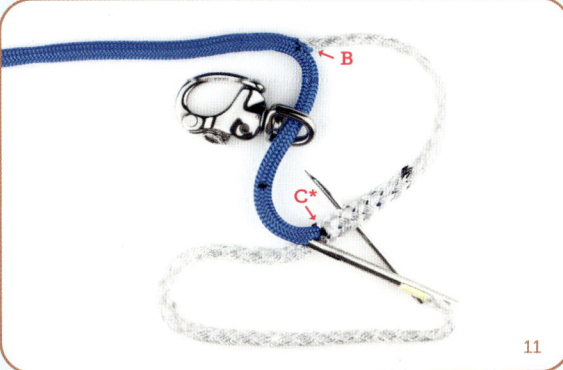

11

Now you are going to insert the thinnest fid possible behind point C* into the cover up to about 10cm past point B.

*For thicker mooring lines, go further down past point B. Rule of thumb: 1cm per mm of line thickness, so for 14mm rope approx 14cm.*

Pull the core all the way through. Once you reach point B, you can let the core slide along the other core with the smooth side of the fid.

*Make sure your fid is not going through the core. If the rope is tightly braided use a soft fid (see Chapter 14) or a pulling needle.*

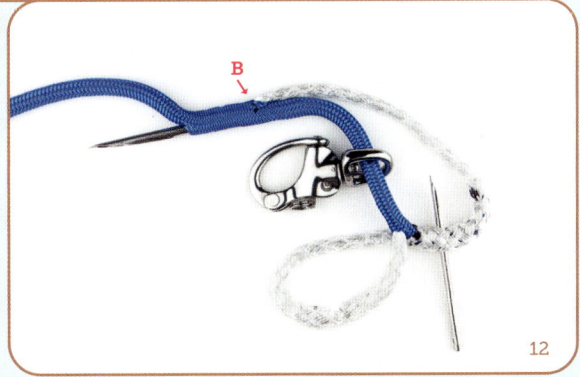

12

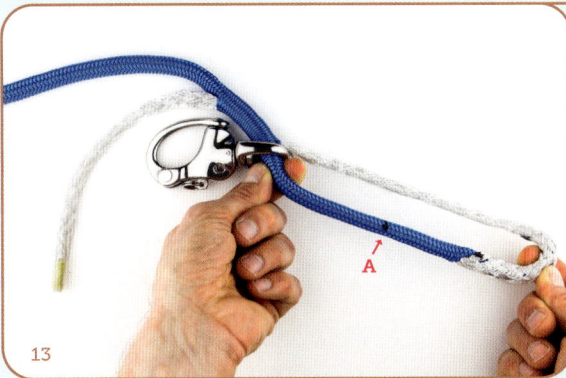

13

Remove the small fid and stretch the loop.

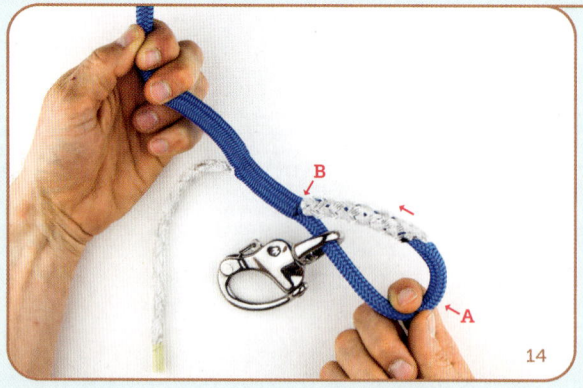

Slide the core back into the cover ('milking') while applying force on the eye until points A and B meet.

Cut the visible piece of core near the cover. Pull on the eye again to make the core disappear completely. In loosely braided ropes, add a whipping behind the eye.

This creates an eye splice in double braid polyester ropes.

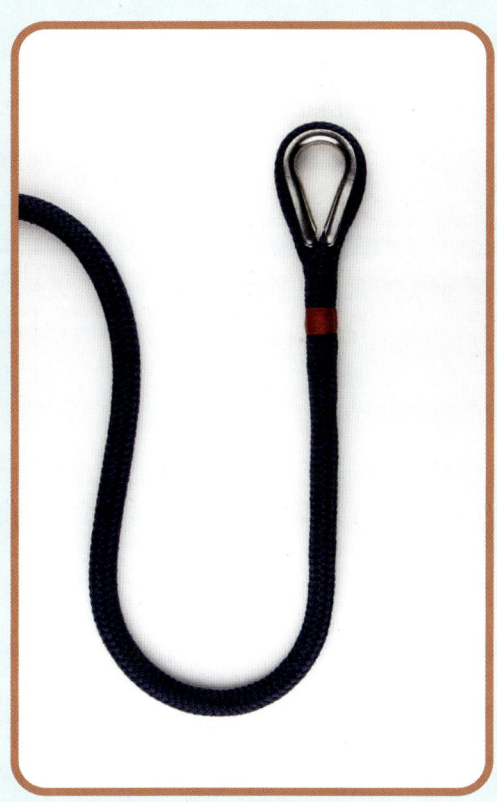

# Stainless steel thimble

If you want to splice in a stainless steel thimble for a mooring line, you can replace steps 2 and 14 with the variations below.

It is advisable to secure the thimble with a whipping.

Step 2 a: Measure the size of the eye according to the size of the thimble.

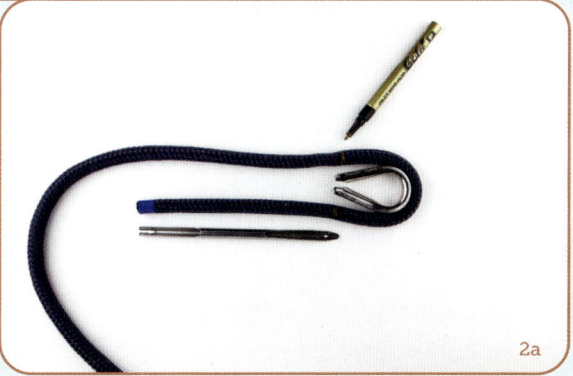

2a

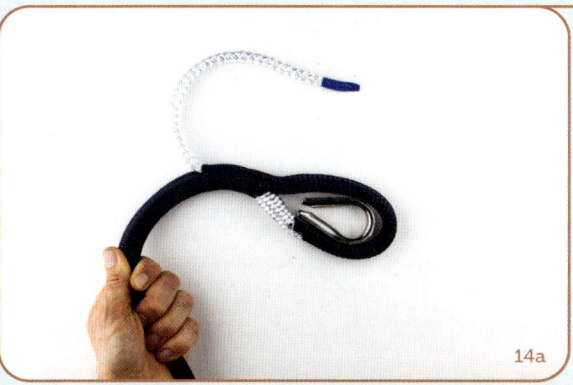

14a

Step 14 a: Make sure the thimble is placed in the loop in time when milking the rope.

# Rope with a laid core

Splicing a rope with a laid core is usually more complicated than double braid polyester ropes. You need more force to take the rope back into itself because there is often less room between the core and the cover. The variations to include a shackle or stainless steel thimble can also be applied here.

Tie a knot about 2 metres into the rope (to keep the core and cover in place). Cut the end off the rope and pull about 10cm of the core out from the cover to create some extra room.

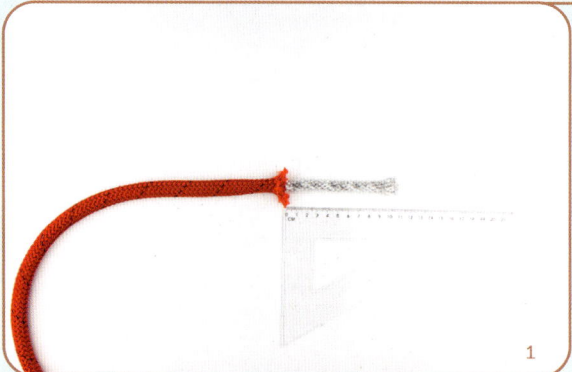

1

Mark point A about 30cm from the end of the cover.

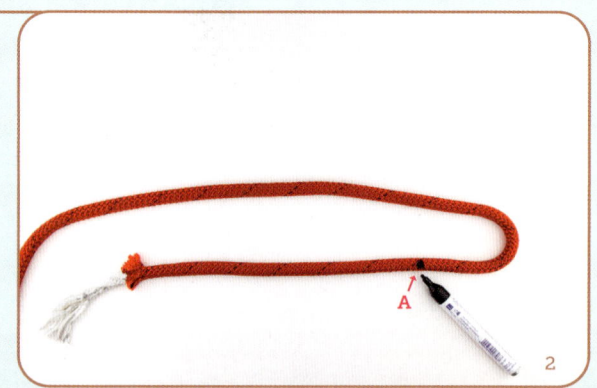

2

Determine the size of the eye and mark point B.

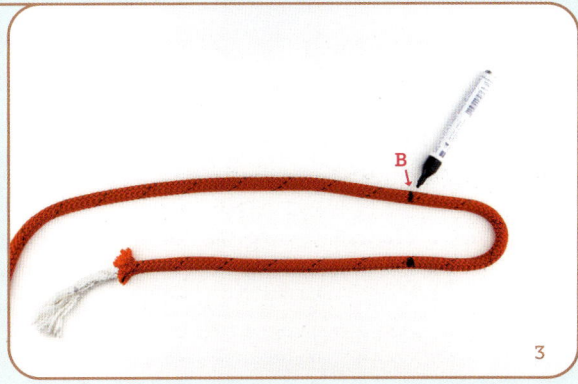

3

Take the core from the cover at point D.

4

Mark point A* on the core (matching point A on the cover).

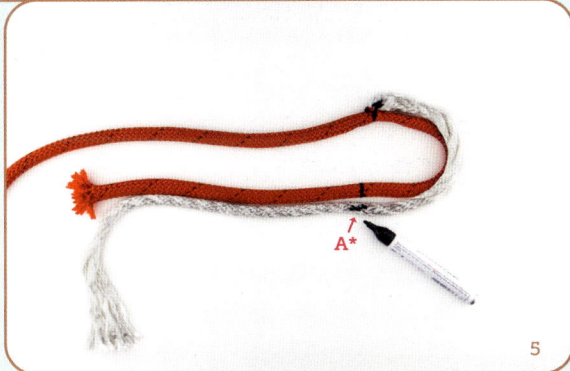

5

Tape the core and unlay the strands at point A*.

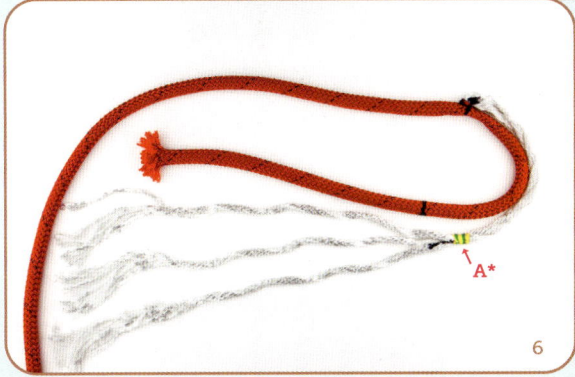

6

Divide the strands into sub-strands.

Cut half of the sub-strands at the point where the tape is. Repeat this for the other two strands. This means you have thinned the core by half from point A* onwards.

Tape the cut strands at point A* so that they are stuck tightly to the rest of the core.

Mark point C opposite the end of the cover (about 30cm from B).

*If you want to splice in a shackle, slide it around the cover now.*

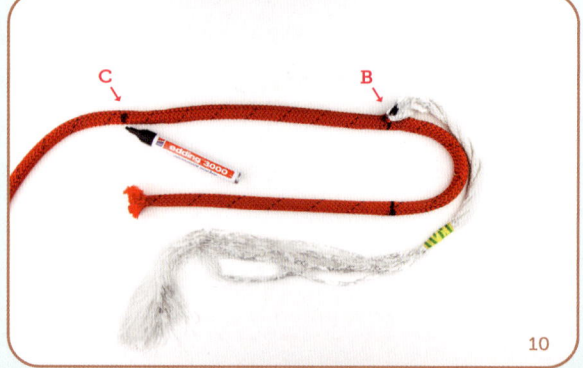

Feed the pulling needle through the core at point C, then along to B and let it emerge at A.

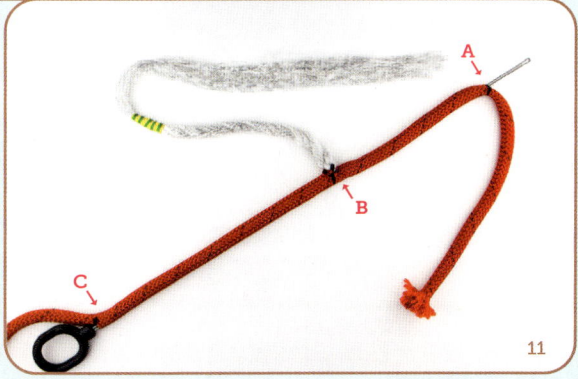

Tuck the core back into the cover.

Pull out the core so that the tape (A*) ends up just beyond B.

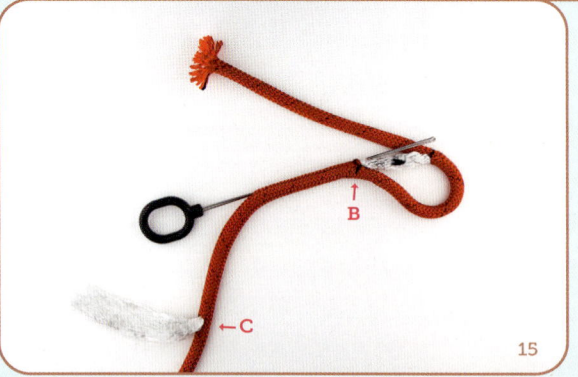

Insert the pulling needle into the cover halfway between B and C (15cm from B). Let it emerge at B.

15

Taper the cover about 2–3cm from point A by cutting some of the strands; use a fid to do this.

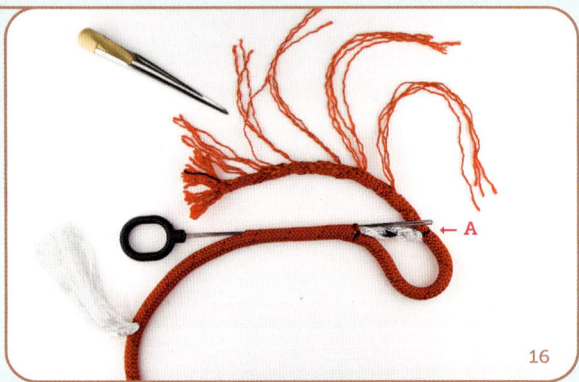

16

Take the tapered cover back into the cover with a pulling needle.

*If the rope is tightly braided use a soft fid (see Chapter 14).*

17

18

Pull on the eye and milk the cover towards the eye.

Pull on the eye again if you have too much cover near the eye.

Mark the visible core, pull it out slightly and cut it.

Pull the cover back slightly by pulling on the eye until you can't see the core any more.

Mark the visible cover at the point where it sticks out.

Pull the visible cover slightly and cut it at the mark.

This creates an eye splice in polyester ropes with a laid core.

# Rope with parallel fibres in the core

A rope with parallel fibres in the core often has a tight inner cover to keep the fibres together. This splice is similar to the one for double braid polyester rope; the main difference is that you cannot take the cover back into the core because the core is not braided.

Cut off the end of the rope to separate the cover from the core. Mark point A at one fid length from the end.

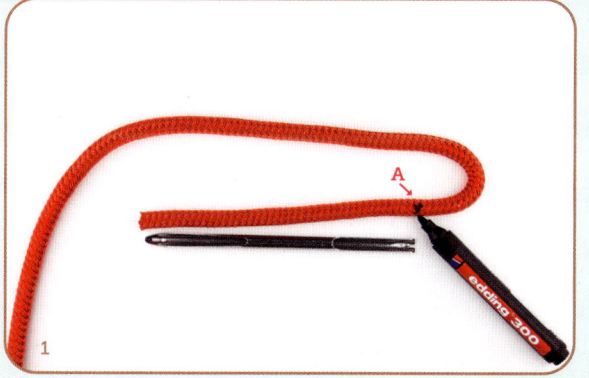

Determine the size of the eye and mark point B opposite A.

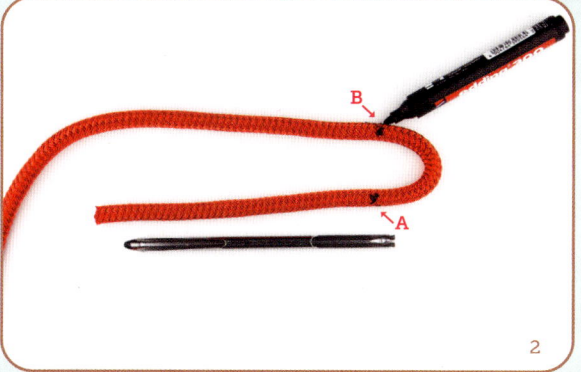

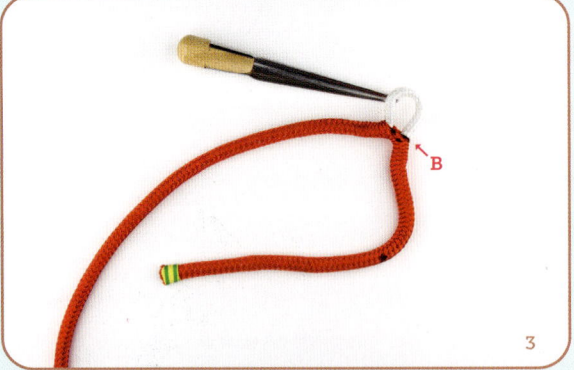

At point B, carefully take out the core from the cover with a thin fid.

Mark the core at the point where it comes out from the cover. This is point B*.

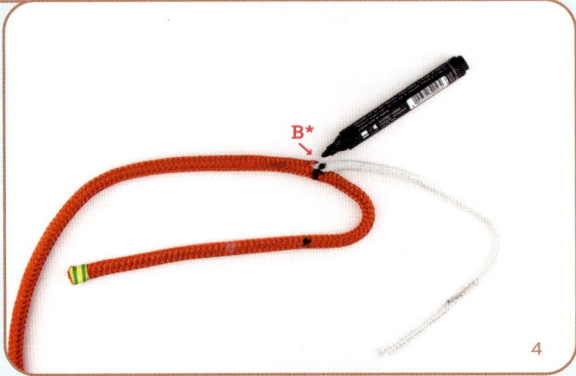

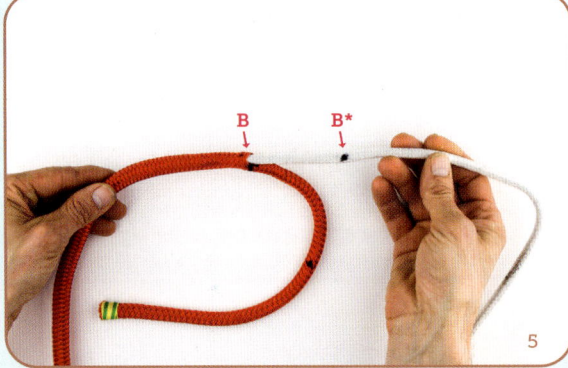

Pull the core further out of the cover at B.

Mark point C* at one fid length from B* going away from the end of the rope.

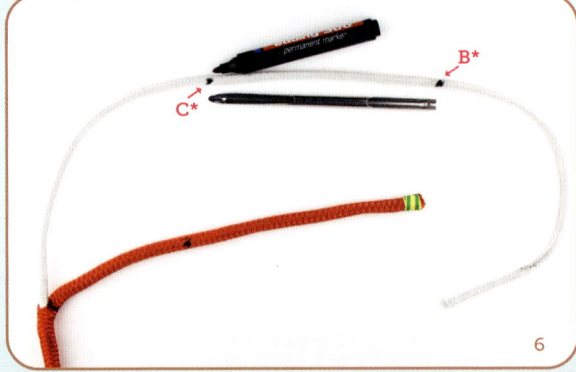

Mark point D* at ¾ of the fid length from C*.

*If you want to splice in a shackle, slide it around the cover now.*

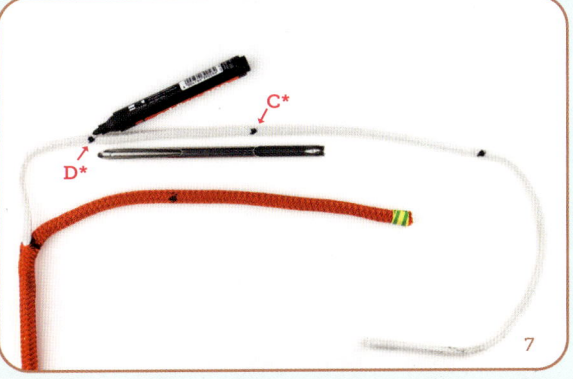

Use as thin a fid as possible to take the core into the cover from the end of the rope.

*Use a soft fid (see Chapter 14) or a pulling needle if the rope is tightly braided.*

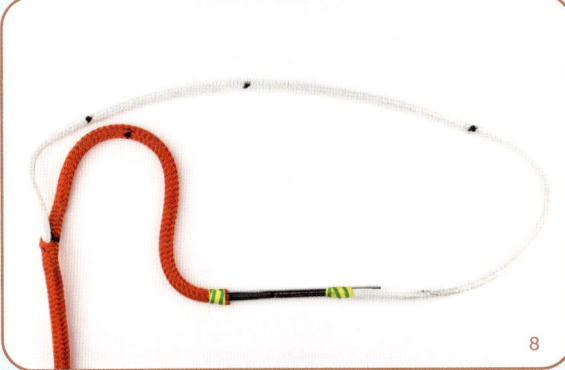

Have the fid come out 5–10cm past point B.

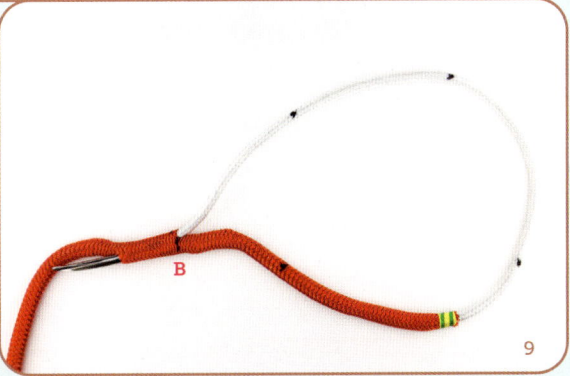

Take the core through point D* and mark a point C at ¾ of the fid length.

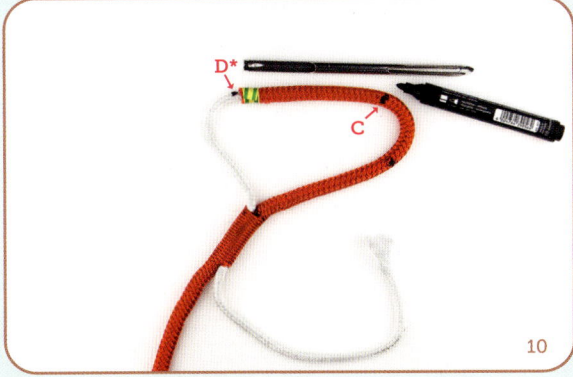

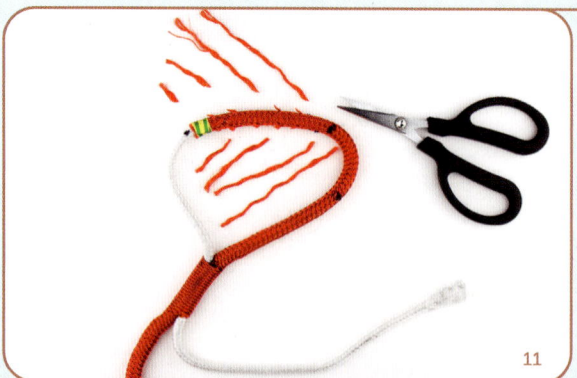

Taper the cover by taking out a few strands and cutting them.

11

Sew the cover to the core from point C to the end of the cover with a few stitches, to prevent it from sliding in the following steps.

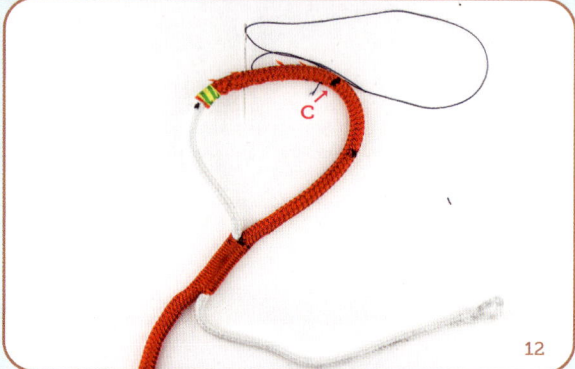

12

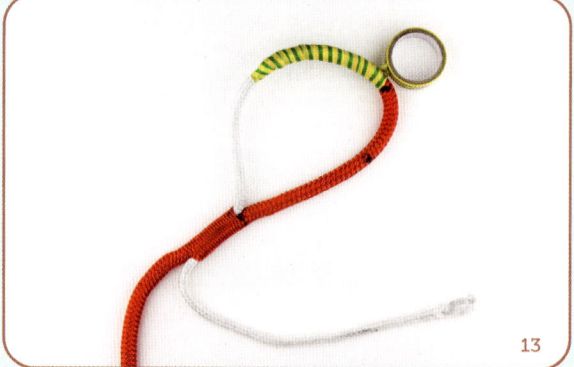

13

Tightly wrap some tape around the rope as shown. Use smooth splicing tape (or regular adhesive tape, which often works even better) so that things don't start to slide in the next step.

Milk the core back into the cover until point A and B meet. If this proves difficult, consult the tips on page 20.

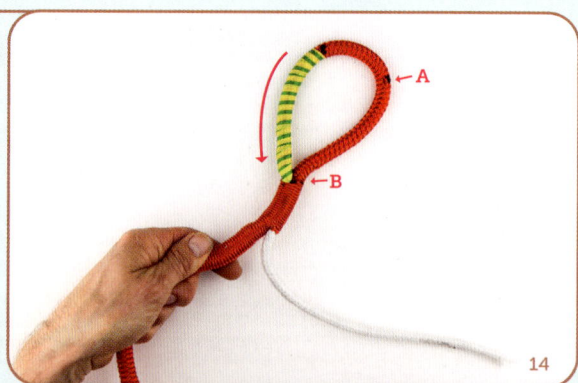

14

Cut the leftover core close to the cover. Pull on the eye once more to make sure the core has disappeared fully.

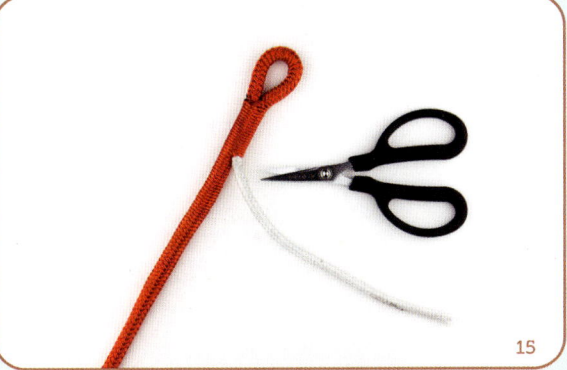

15

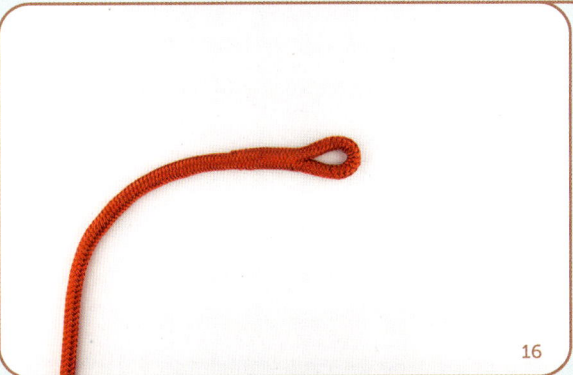

16

This creates an eye splice in a polyester rope with parallel fibres in the core.

# 7 Eye splice in Dyneema ropes

The principle of a Dyneema eye is a core-to-core splice, in which a length of at least 60 times the diameter of the rope is taken back into itself. Several sources recommend using 50–70 times the diameter for coated Dyneema. Avient advises using 60 times the diameter for coated Dyneema, and 100 times the diameter for uncoated Dyneema. For a 6mm coated rope that would mean 36cm.

If you want to splice in a stainless steel thimble with Dyneema, you need a thimble that is closed on the narrow side. It is not possible to crush this thimble so it can withstand much higher forces.

## Single braid rope

This chapter starts with the basic method for splicing Dyneema. This is very simple. You put the line back into itself at least 60 times its diameter. Under tension, the end, which is inserted into the line, is clamped by the outer part of the line. The eye remains firmly in place. However, if the line is not under tension, then you can pull the eye right out. That is why you lock the splice. Locking can be done with a stitched whipping as seen in the 'basic method', or with a 'lock splice'. All techniques are equally strong. The methods for single braid Dyneema can also be used for single braid polyester ropes, such as those used for lazy jacks.

## Basic method

Mark point A at 60 times the rope's diameter (at least 24cm for a 4mm rope).

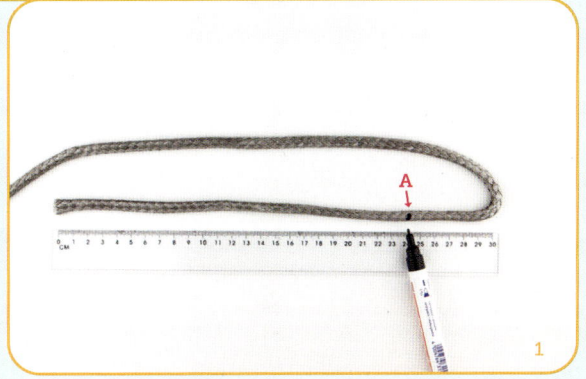

Determine the size of the eye and mark point B.

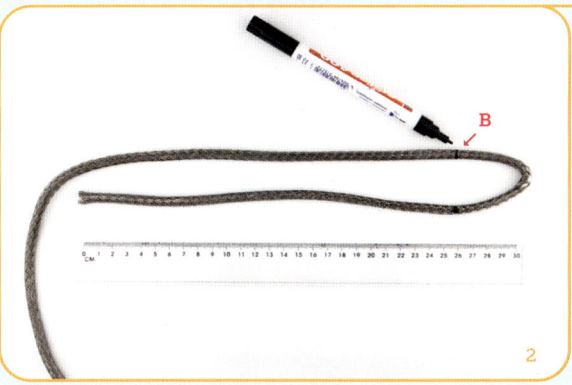

Insert a fid into the rope at point B.

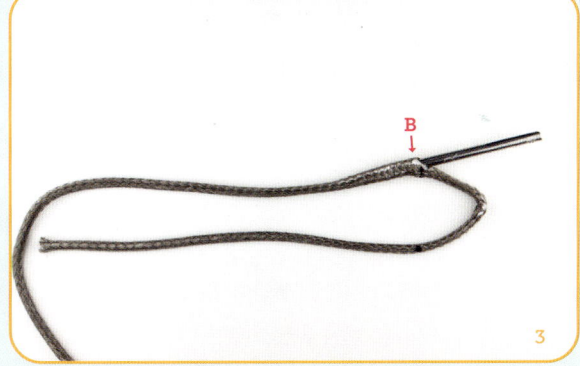

Pull the short end of the rope through so that it disappears completely.

Pull the end of the line and remove some strands from the short end.

Cut the loose strands so that the rope becomes thinner ('tapering').

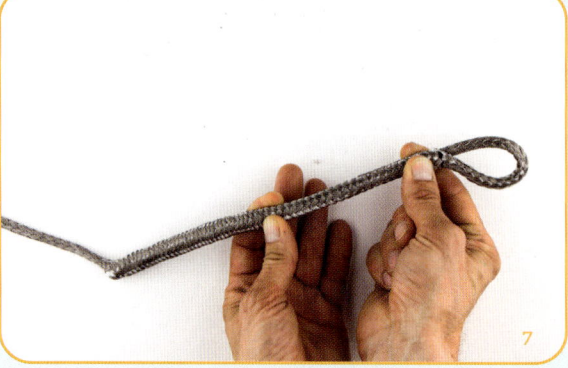

Shape the eye back to the original size, hold it and slide the outer rope over the inner.

Add a stitched whipping (page 164) to prevent the eye from moving when it is not under tension.

This completes the basic method to make an eye splice in single braid Dyneema rope.

## Method for hollow braid with a grip fibre

A rope made up of a hollow braid with a grip fibre (such as Swiftcord) is spliced just as in the basic method above. The only difference is that you taper the rope before you take it back into itself, because this rope is more tightly braided than single braid Dyneema and therefore has less space inside.

Follow steps 1 and 2 of the basic method above, then:

Taper two thirds of the length between A and the end of the rope.

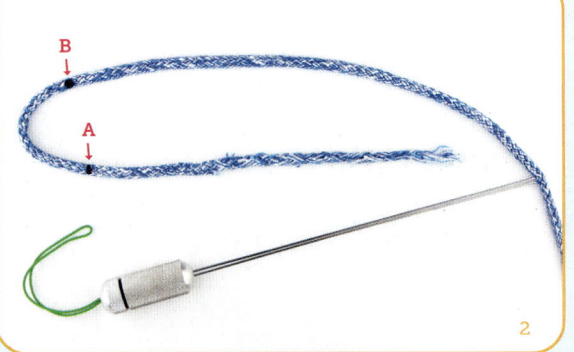

Fold the rope and insert the pulling needle as shown, about a third further from B than the distance between A and the end of the rope (30cm for a 4mm rope).

Take the tapered end back through. Follow steps 7 and 8 of the basic method above).

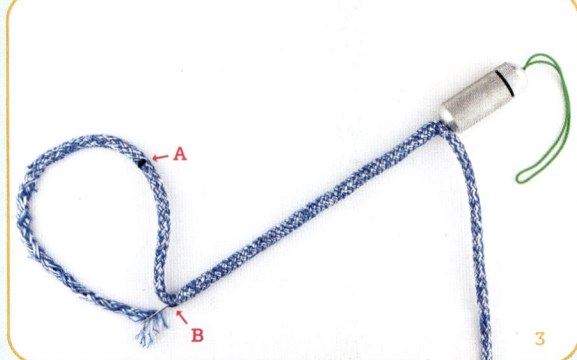

This creates an eye splice in a hollow braid with a grip fibre.

# Lock splice

If possible, lock the size of the eye with a so-called lock splice (or Brummel splice), as is explained below. There are two methods, one for a rope with two loose ends and one for a rope with one end free and one that's attached.

# Lock splice –
# Two loose ends

Mark point A at 60 times the rope diameter (30cm for a 5mm rope).

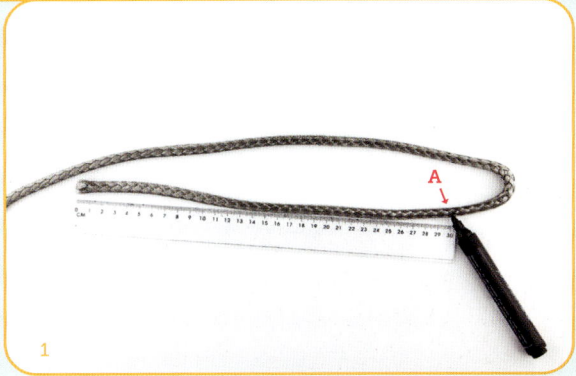

Determine the size of the eye and mark point B.

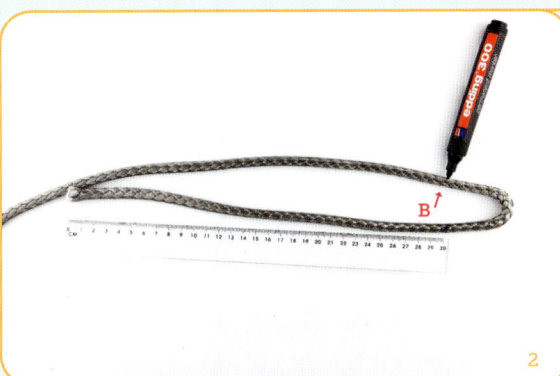

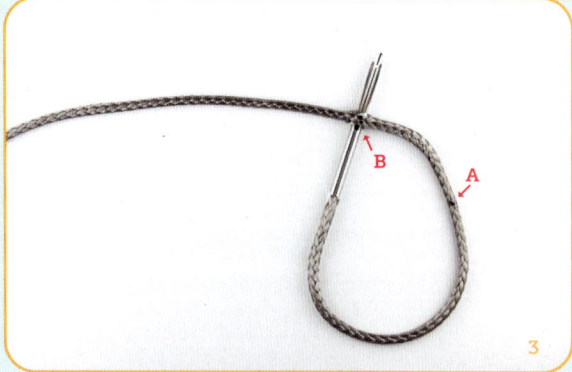

Push a fid right through the core at point B. Make sure you have the same number of strands on either side.

3

Pull the short end through until points A and B meet.

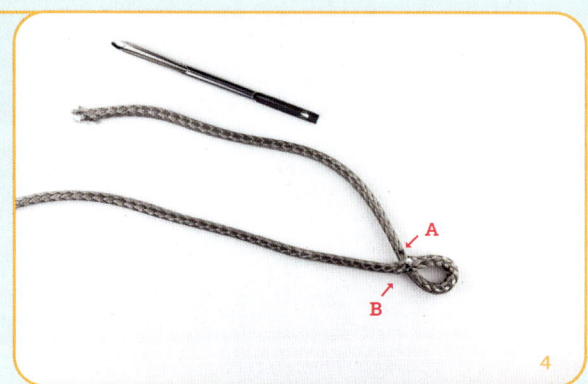

4

Insert a fid behind the eye at point A as shown.

5

Take the longer end of the rope through point A completely. If this longer end is fixed, continue with step 5 on page 66.

6

The splice is now locked; the eye can't be pulled out any more.

Option 1: Insert the fid just behind the eye. Pull the short end of the rope through so that it disappears completely.

Option 2: It is often easier to use a pulling needle here, particularly for thin ropes.

Pull out the fid with the rope to expose more of the inner rope.

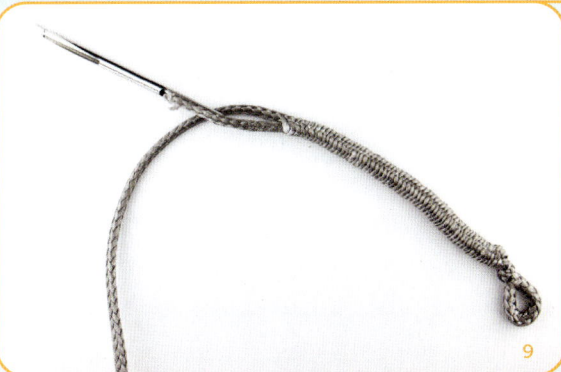

Unlay some strands from the tail.

10

Cut the strands to taper the end.

11

Hold the eye and slide the outer rope back over the inner one.

12

This creates a lock splice in single braid Dyneema.

13

# Lock splice – one end attached

If you want a lock splice in a rope that is attached on one side, follow these instructions:

Mark point A at 60 times the rope's diameter (30cm for a 5mm rope).

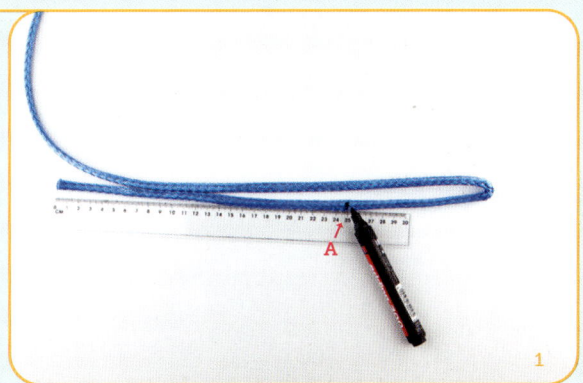

Determine the size of the eye and mark point B.

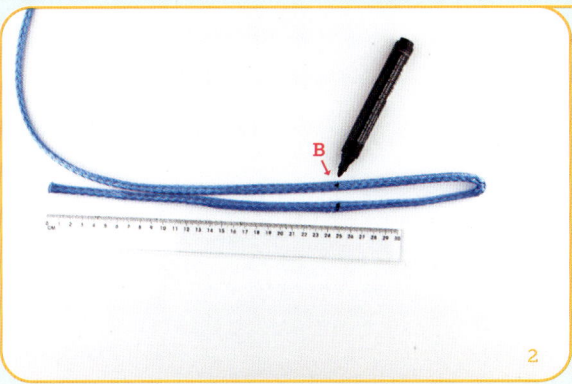

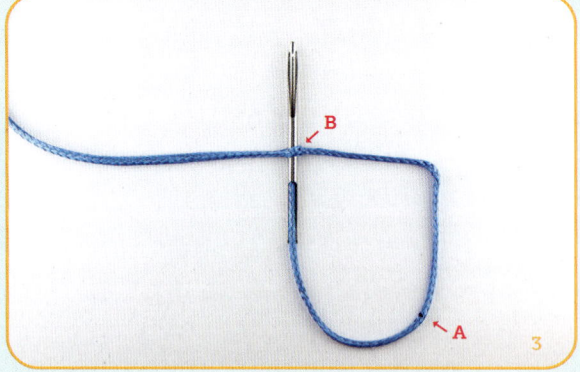

Insert a fid right through the core at point B. Make sure you have the same number of strands on either side of the fid.

Take the short end through until points A and B meet.

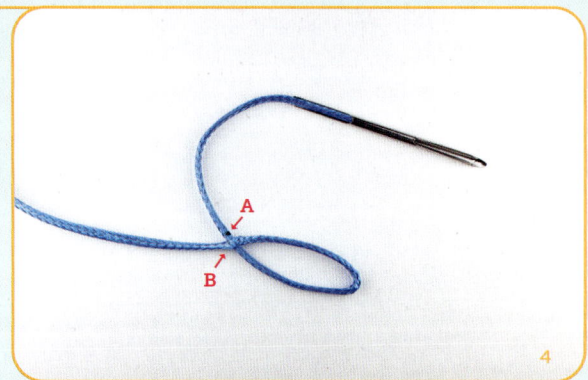

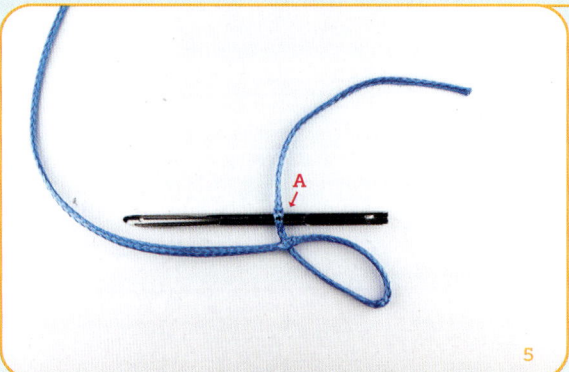

Insert a thicker fid in the short end at A.

Now pull the eye through point A.

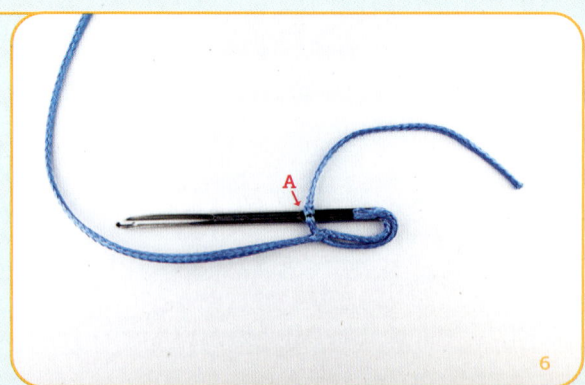

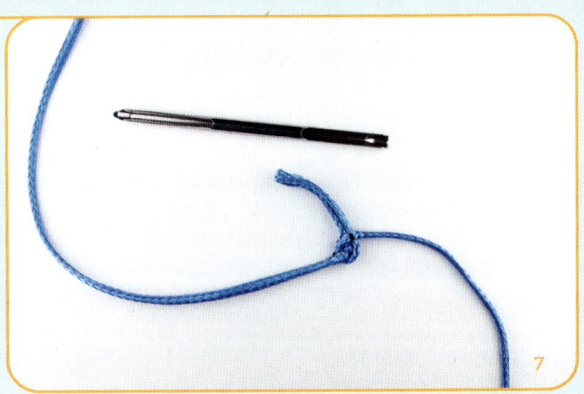

If you pull the eye through tightly you'll get a twist in the rope at point A. If you want to leave it this way, continue with step 12.

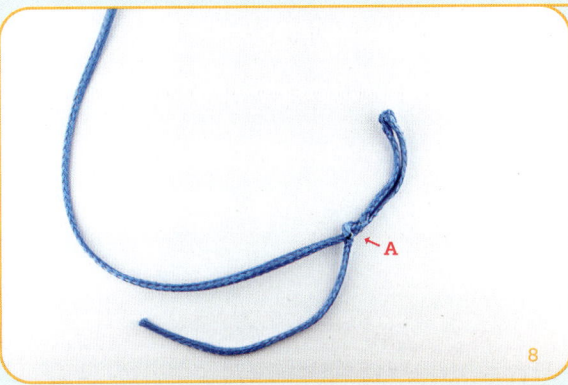

Remove the twist by turning back the loose end at point A.

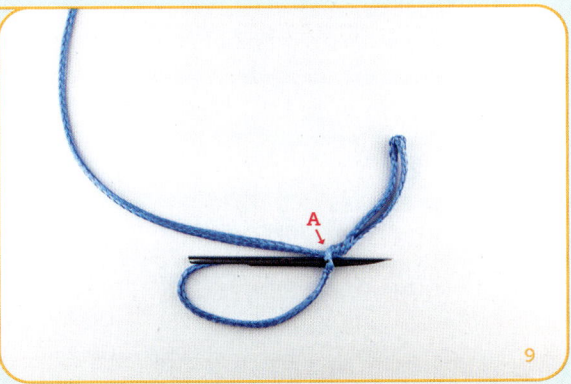

Pull the rope through completely.

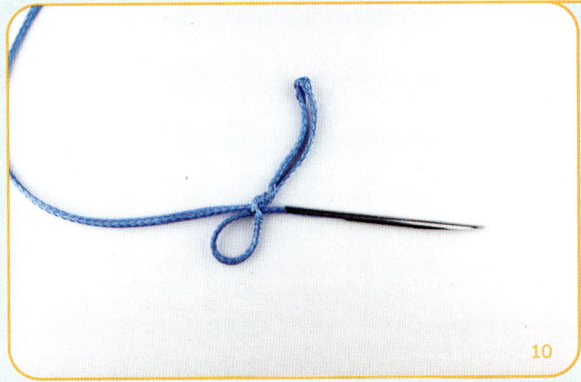

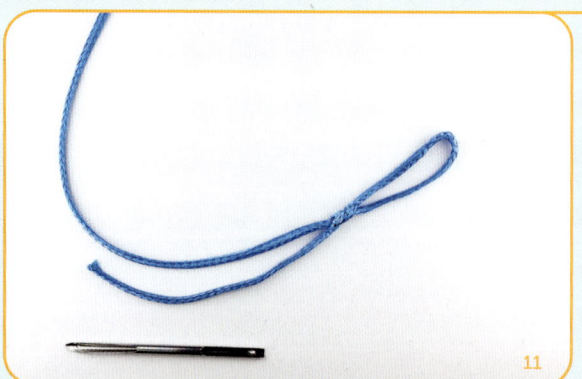

The twist is now gone and the lock is in place.

11

Insert the fid just behind the eye. Pull the short end of the rope through until it disappears completely (use a pulling needle for thin ropes).

12

13

Pull out the fid with the rope to expose more of the inner rope.

Unlay some strands from the tail.

14

Cut the loose strands to taper the end.

15

16

Hold the eye and slide the outer rope back over the inner one.

This creates a lock splice in single braid Dyneema where one side of the rope is attached.

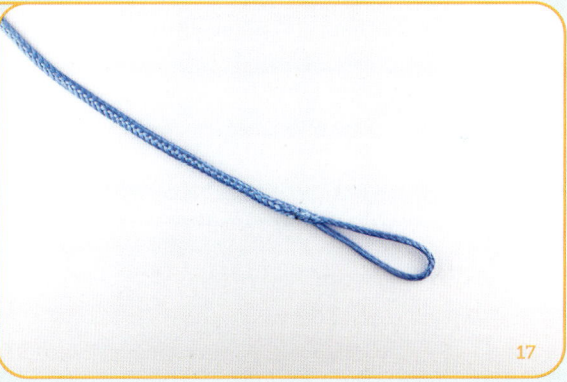

17

# Lock splice – One end attached fixing a thimble

You cannot use the technique described in the previous section to splice a thimble or low friction ring to the rope. After all, you can't put the entire ring through the line in step 6. But you can use the following technique to make a splice where the rope tightens itself around the ring.

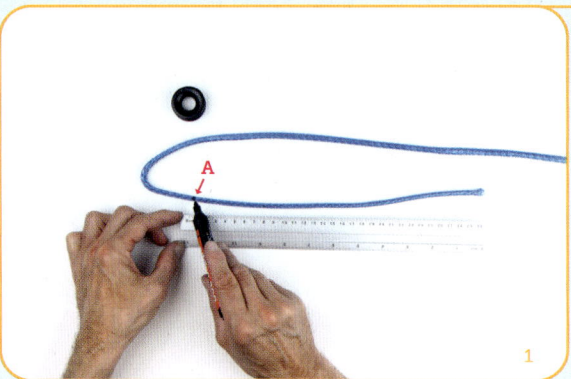

Mark point A at 60 times the rope's diameter (30 cm for a 5mm rope).

Insert a thicker fid at A through the rope. Fold the line in half and pull it through the line.

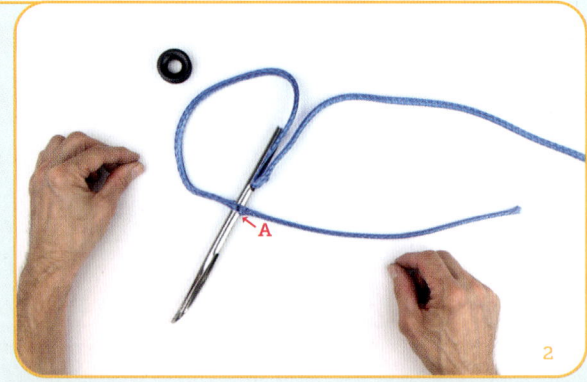

If you pull the folded line through you will get a twist in the rope.

Remove the twist by turning back the loose end at point A.

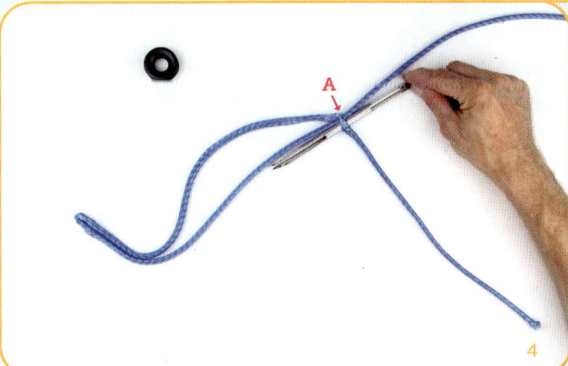

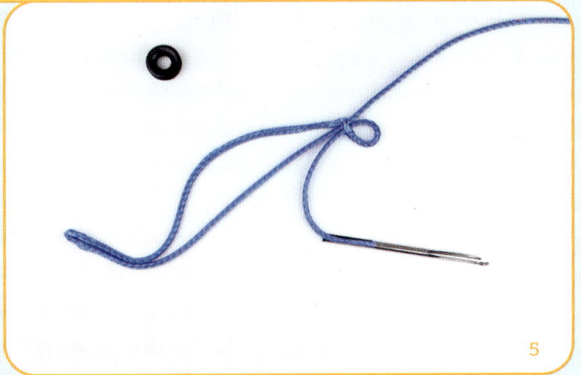

Put the ring in the eye and pull the fixed end. The rope will pull tightly around the eye. Follow steps 12 through 16 of the previous section to complete the splice.

# Double braid rope

Dyneema is very UV resistant and the polyester cover does not contribute to the strength of the rope. You therefore splice only the core so the techniques described below are very similar to those for single braid Dyneema. If the rope has an aramid fibre core, such as Kevlar, then you do need to splice the cover as well to protect against UV (see page 78).

## Without using the cover

There are two methods for this, both of which create equally strong splices. In both, the core is spliced in the same way as the core of single braid Dyneema (see pages 60 and 64). The easiest method, where the cover is kept in place with a whipping, is explained first. The second method requires a little bit more work; the cover is laid around the eye.

## Method 1: cover attached with a whipping (easy)

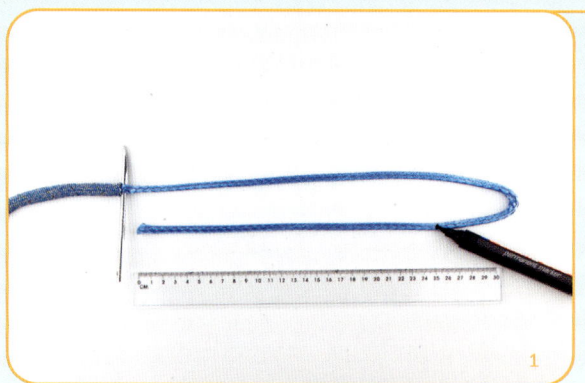

Pull out the core from the cover and secure it with a thin fid.

Create a lock splice. Depending on your preference and the situation, you can choose the lock splice for two loose ends (see page 61) or the one with one end attached (see page 65).

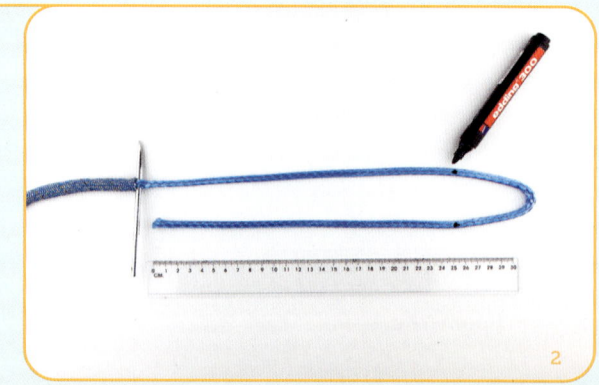

Once the eye is finished, milk the cover back to the eye.

Secure the cover with a stitched whipping.

Milk the spare cover to the other side.

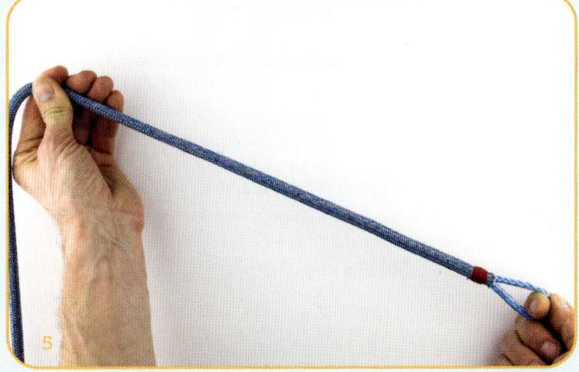

Cut the spare cover.

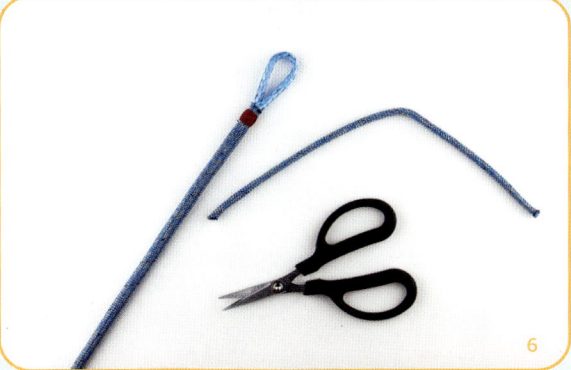

# Method 2: cover taken back over the eye splice

This splice is as strong as the previous one but has a slightly nicer finish.

Pull out the core 5–10cm from the cover to create more room. Rule of thumb for this 'overlength' is 1cm for each mm rope thickness, so 8cm for an 8mm rope. Mark point A at a minimum of 60 times the core diameter from the end (36cm for a 6mm core). A–B determines the size of the eye.

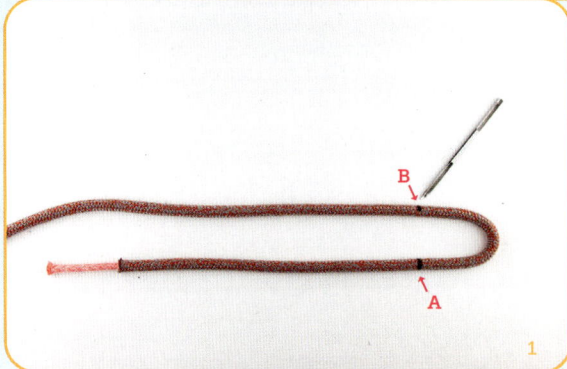

Take out the core from the cover at B and mark it B*. Pull the core further out of the cover to create enough space for making the splice. Secure the core at the point where it comes out of the cover with a small fid.

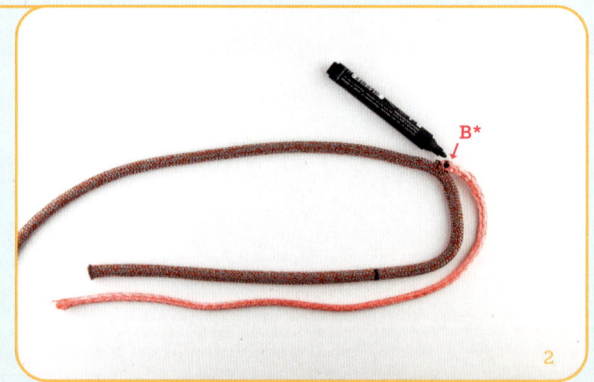

Create a lock splice. Depending on your preference and situation, choose either the lock splice for two loose ends (see page 61) or the one with one end attached (see page 65).

Insert a pulling needle about 5cm through the cover next to the core. You could taper the end of the cover before it is taken back into itself.

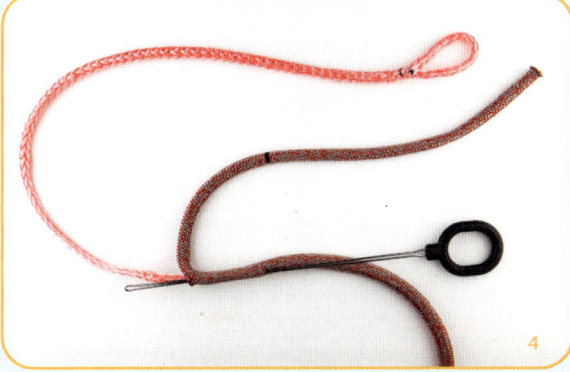

Take the end of the cover through the eye and pull it back into itself. Do that at the point where there is only a single core because this is where you will have space for it. Make sure the cover is not twisted.

If the rope is tightly braided use a soft fid (see Chapter 14).

Milk the core back into the cover.

This step can be hard; if needed use a hammer to loosen the fibres.

When milking the cover over the thicker part of the cover, simultaneously pull on the loop and slide over the cover. If necessary, attach a shackle to the eye and apply a bit of tension with a winch.

Pull the cover through around the core until you see only the Dyneema eye.

Cut the cover and put tension on the eye again to make the end disappear into the cover.

Secure with a stitched whipping to prevent the cover from slipping off.

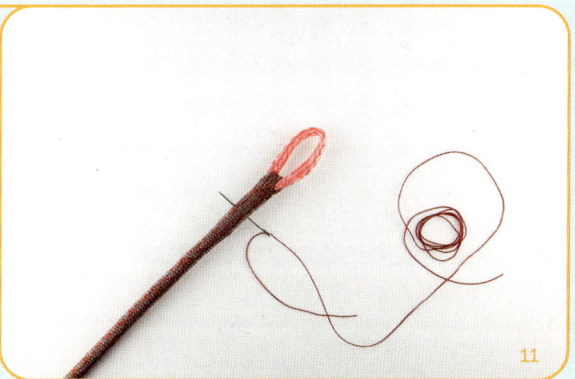

This creates an eye splice in double braid Dyneema rope, with the cover taken back around the eye.

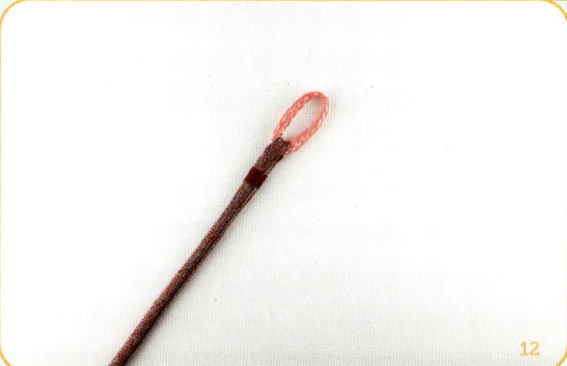

## Using the cover

While you don't need to use the cover with Dyneema, you should also splice the cover if the core is made of aramid or Vectran fibres, to protect against UV damage. This splice is fairly difficult because the cover will get very tight and you'll need a lot of force.

Beginners are advised to use one of the lock splice methods described above (page 72 or 74) if they are splicing a double braid Dyneema rope.

Mark point A at 60 times the core's diameter (36cm for a 6mm core). Mark point B; the distance from A to B determines the size of the eye.

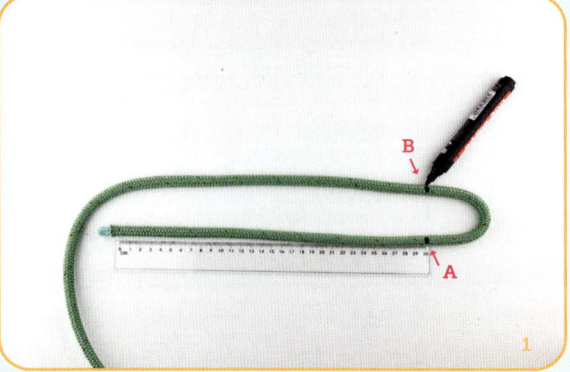

Take the core out of the cover at point A and mark it.

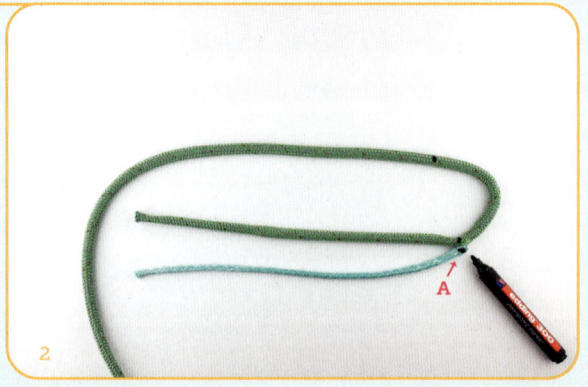

Make some extra room in the cover by taking out 5–10cm of the core. Rule of thumb for this 'overlength' is 1cm for each mm rope thickness, so 8cm for an 8mm rope. This point is called A*.

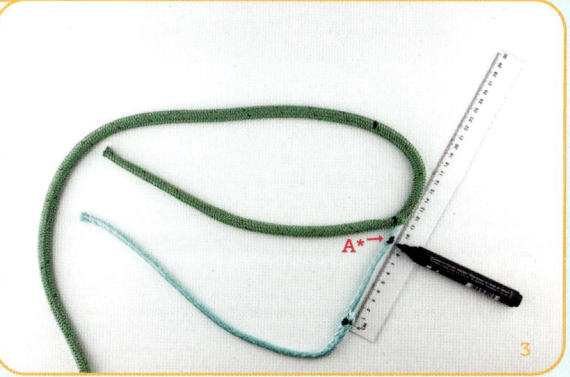

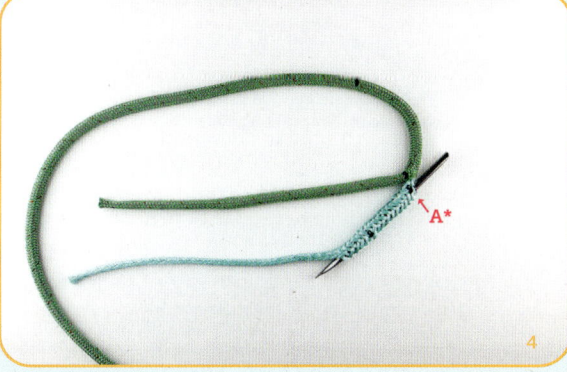

Insert a fid into point A* and let it emerge about 12cm further down.

Pull the cover through.

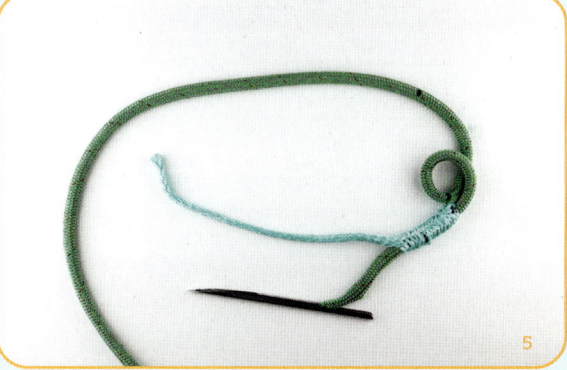

Mark the cover where it emerges.

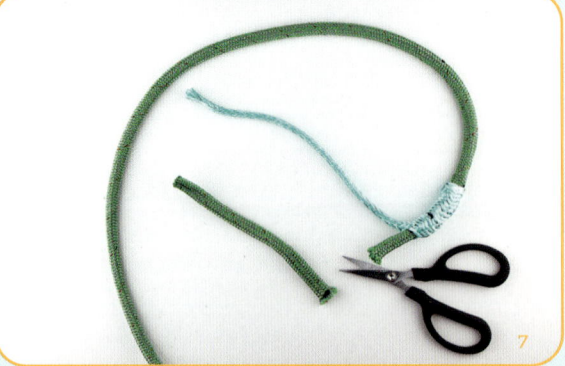

Cut the cover at the mark.

Taper the cover by cutting it off diagonally.

Slide the core over the tapered cover.

Take the core out of the cover at point B.

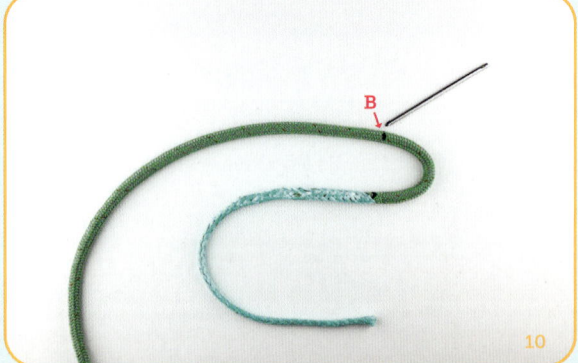

B

Make a big loop by pulling out
the core.

Stretch the cover tightly around
the core.

Insert a fid upwards into the core
at point B.

Take the end of the core back
into itself.

Take the fid far enough in so that the core completely disappears inside itself.

15

Optional: secure the core and cover in place with a few stitches to prevent them from moving.

16

17

Taper the core by cutting it diagonally.

Slide the core back around itself to create an even loop. It is important to fully stretch out the core before you start with the next step.

18

Milk the cover over the core towards the eye.

This step can be difficult; use a hammer to loosen the fibres.

When milking the thicker part of the core, simultaneously pull on the loop and slide over the cover. If necessary, attach a shackle to the eye and apply a bit of tension with a winch.

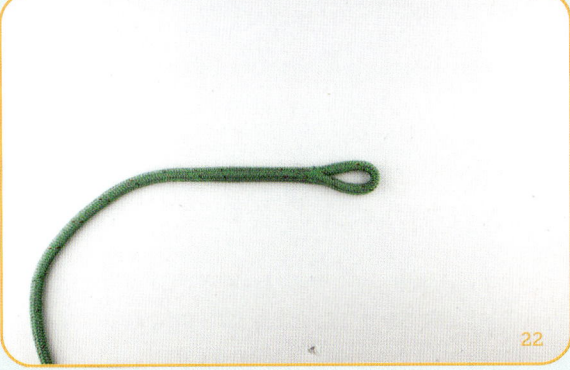

This creates an eye splice including the cover in double braid ropes with high-performance fibres.

# Double layer cover

This splice will be the same as the one for double braid Dyneema above, from step 7 onwards. The only difference is that the inner cover needs to be removed. This inner cover does not add any strength to the rope and is merely a 'filler'. This provides more room in the cover, which means you need less force and the area with the core taken back into itself stays flexible. You determine the length of inner cover you need to remove in steps 1–3.

Cut a piece off the end and take out the core with the inner cover. Mark point A at 60 times the core diameter.

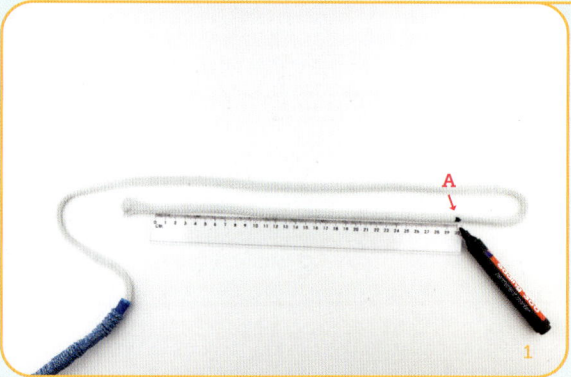

Mark point B, depending on the size of eye you want.

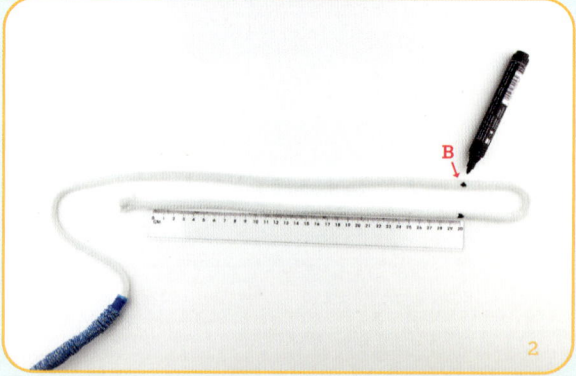

Fold the rope and mark point C on the longer end, 10cm past the shorter end.

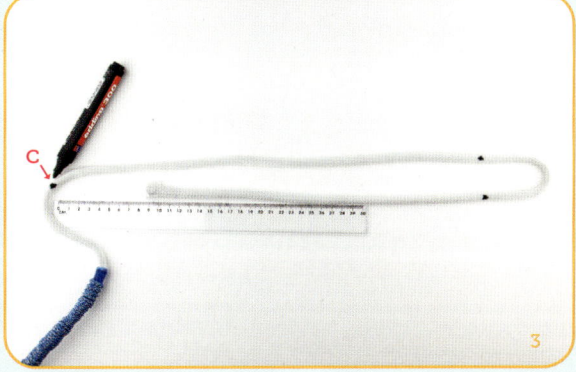

Remove the inner cover at point C. This is much easier if you bunch it up as much as possible. Make sure you don't damage the core when cutting.

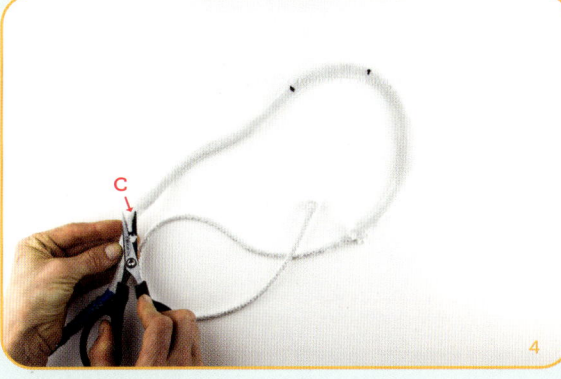

The inner cover is now removed.

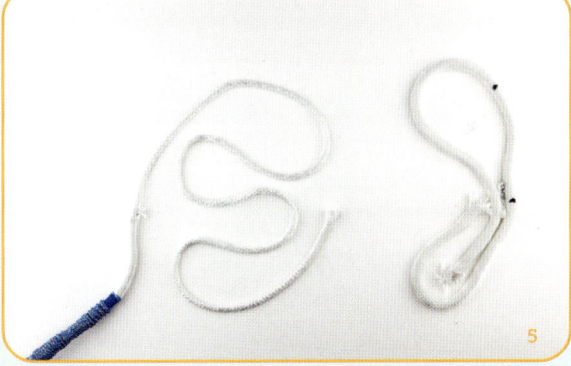

Slide the cover completely back over the core.

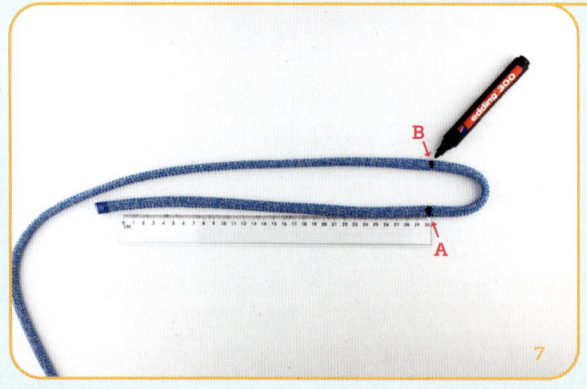

You marked points A and B earlier in step 1 and 2 to know at which point to remove the inner cover. Mark the same points A and B on the cover.

Take the core from the cover at A and mark it.

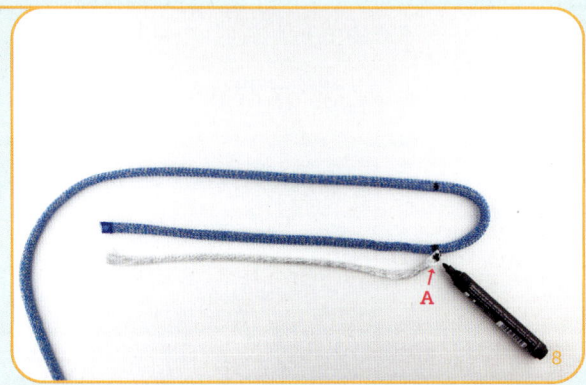

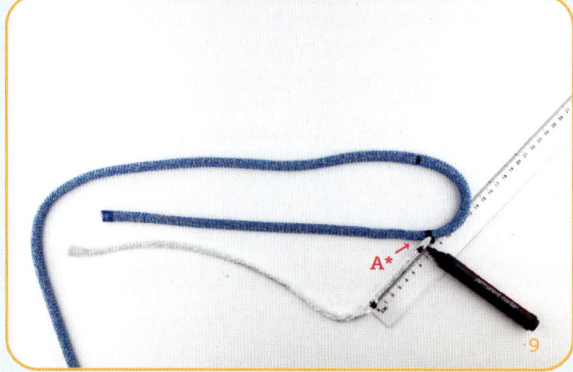

Create more room in the cover by taking out 5–10cm of the core. The rule of thumb for this 'overlength' is 1cm for each mm rope thickness, so 8cm for an 8mm rope. Mark this point A*.

Insert a fid into point A* and let it emerge out about 12cm further down.

Pull through the cover.

Mark the cover at the point where it emerges.

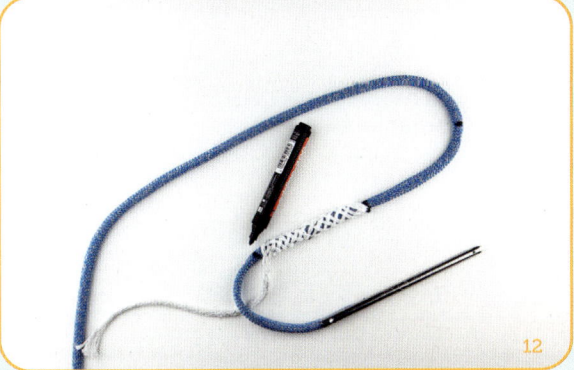

Cut the cover at the mark.

Taper the cover by cutting it diagonally.

Slide the core back over the tapered cover.

Take out the core from the cover at point B.

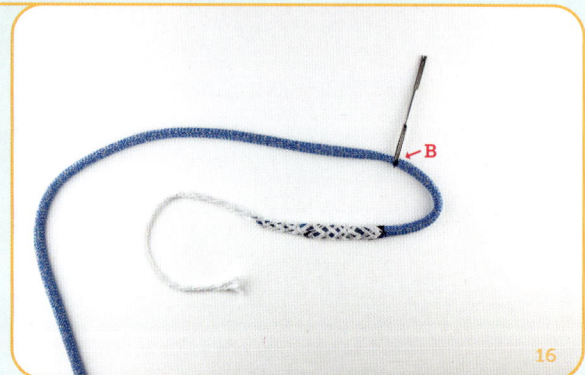

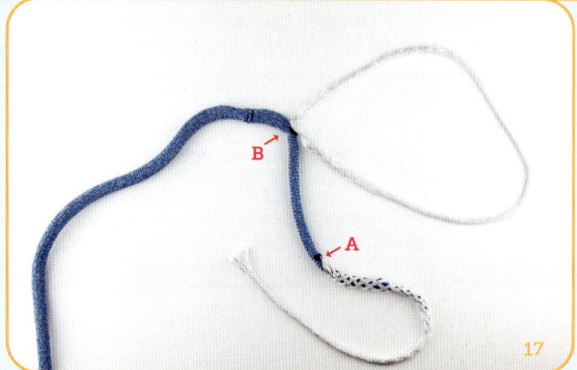

Make a big loop by pulling the core out. Pull the cover tight around the core from point A to point B.

Insert a fid upwards into the core at point B.

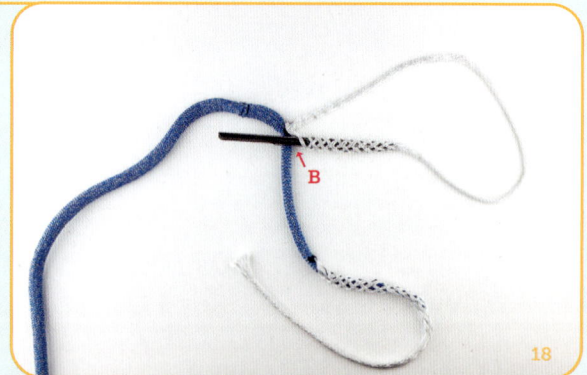

Take the end of the core through the core.

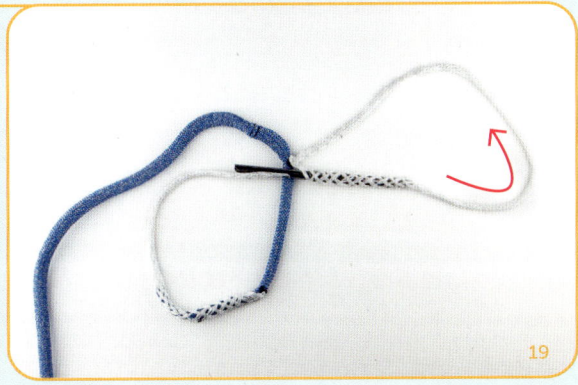

Let the fid emerge from the core at such a distance that the cover can disappear inside itself completely.

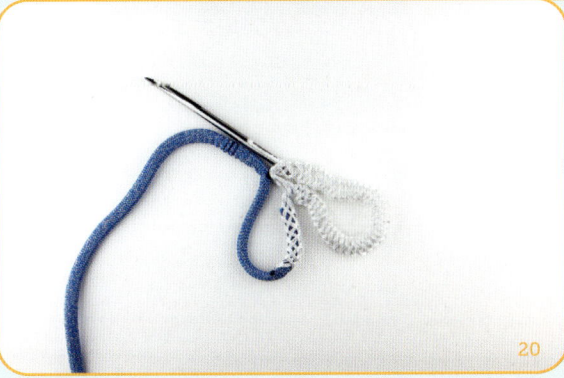

Optional: secure the core and cover in place with a few stitches so that they can't move.

Taper the core by cutting it diagonally.

Slide the core from the loop to cover the tapered part. It is important to fully stretch out the core before you start with the next step.

Milk the cover over the core (towards the edge). Add a stitched whipping below the eye if you like.

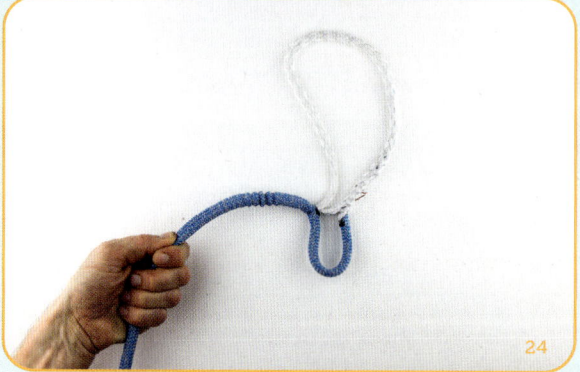

This creates an eye splice in double braid Dyneema with a double-layered cover.

# 8 Dyneema shackles

## Soft shackles

Soft shackles are strong, light and safe and are increasingly replacing stainless steel shackles. Not only are soft shackles lighter, they also prevent damage to the boat and crew. Soft shackles are stronger than the breaking load of the original rope because the rope is doubled up. To close the shackle you use a soft shackle knot or diamond knot, as explained on page 105.

Vary and experiment with the size of the soft shackles. I usually use about 85cm of rope for a 4mm shackle. For an additional 1mm in diameter you'll roughly need an extra 10cm of rope.

## Soft shackle Type 1

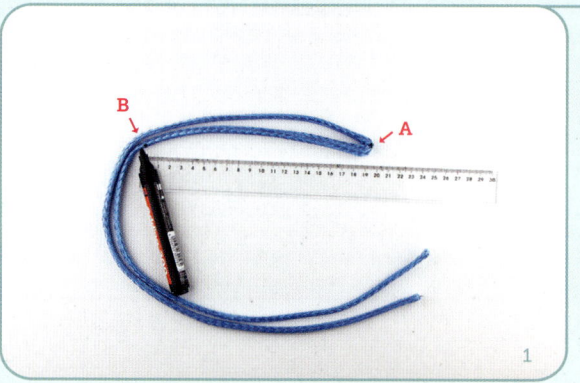

Mark point A in the middle of the rope and point B to determine the size of the shackle. This should be about 20cm from the centre for a 4mm rope.

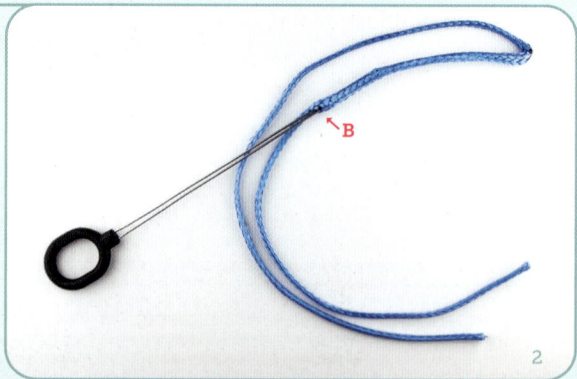

Insert a pulling needle into point B.

Take out the needle at point A.

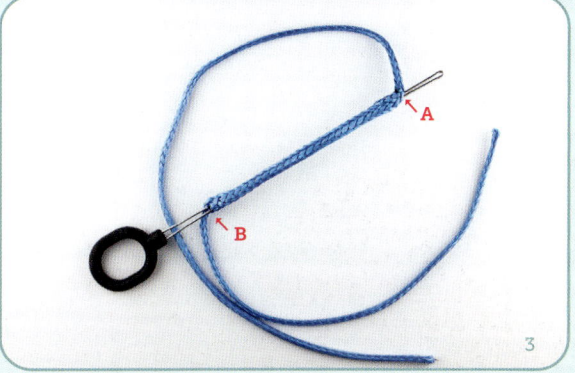

Clamp the long end in the needle and pull it back

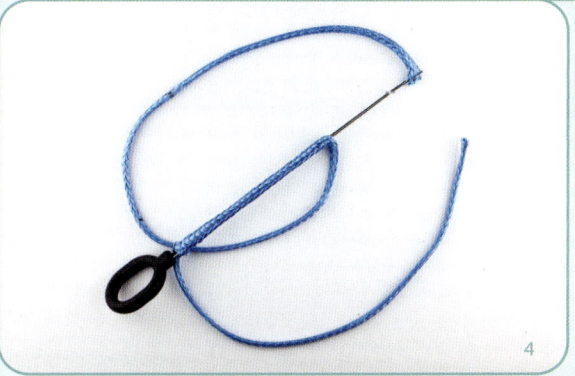

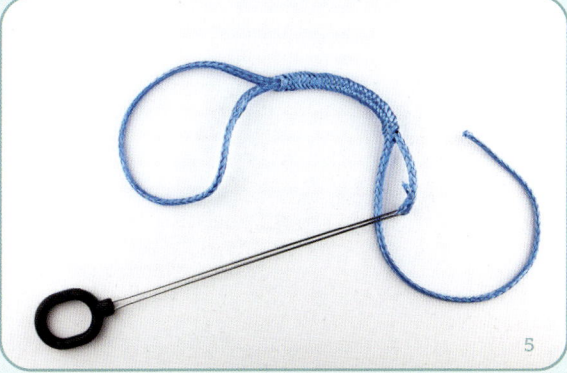

Feed a round abject through the loop and stretch the rope.

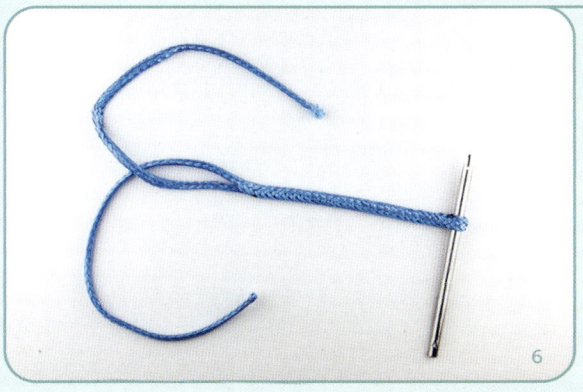

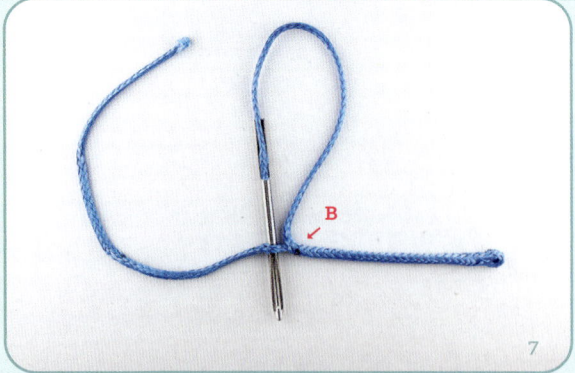

Lock the shackle by taking the outer rope through the inner rope behind point B.

B

7

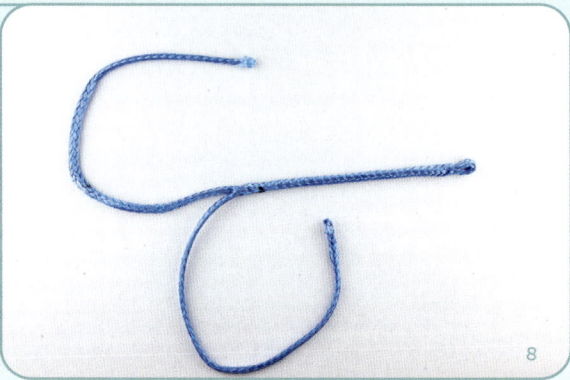

8

Tie the soft shackle knot with both ends, using the method on page 105, and cut both ends.

9

Make the eye of the soft shackle as large as possible. Take a thin rope and feed it through the inner rope.

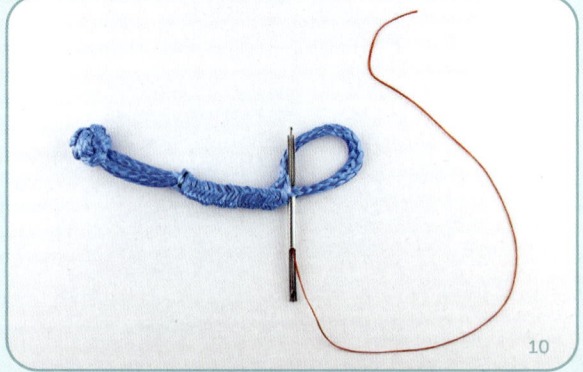

10

Have both ends of the quick-release string visible and close up the soft shackle. Tie a knot in the thin rope and the soft shackle is finished.

The quick-release string is used to open the eye.

This creates a Dyneema soft shackle, type 1.

# Soft shackle
# Type 2

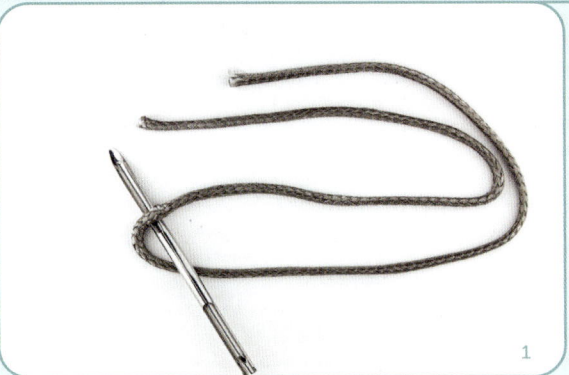

Fold the rope and take a fid right through the rope just next to the centre.

Take the longest end through the rope.

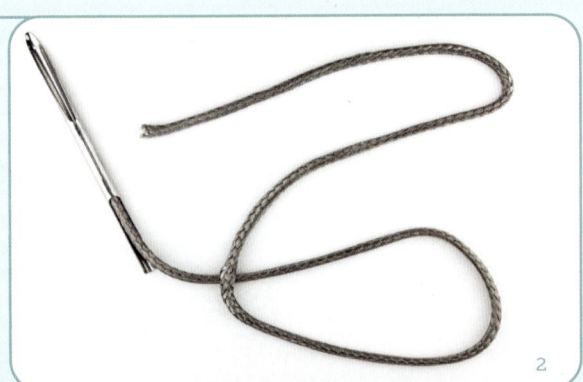

Determine the size of the soft shackle and mark point A. This would be at about 20cm for a 4mm rope.

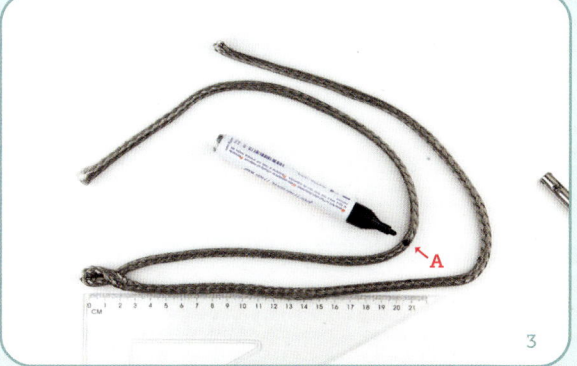

3

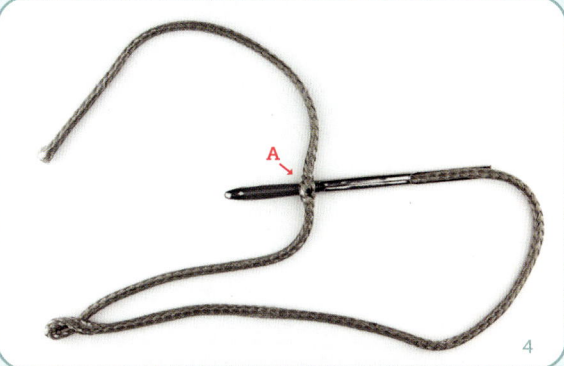

4

Take one end through point A, as shown.

Take the other end through the rope just behind point A.

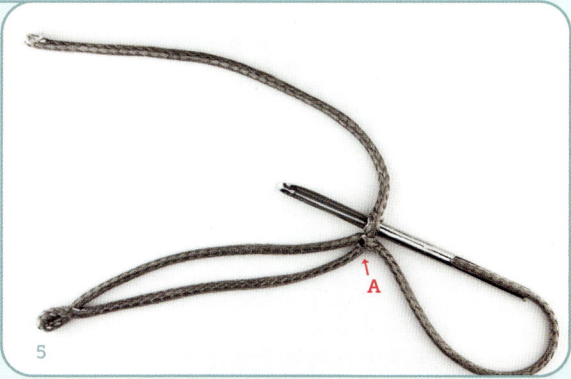

5

6

The splice is now locked.

Tie the soft shackle knot with both ends, using the method on page 105, and cut both ends.

7

Open the eye and place it over the knot.

8

This creates a Dyneema soft shackle, type 2.

9

# Soft shackle integrated

This splice shows how you can combine techniques from this book. A combination of the soft shackle on page 92 with a double braid Dyneema eye splice on page 74 will give you a soft shackle that is integral to the rope. This is something for the more advanced splicer.

Take 5–10cm of the core from the cover. Rule of thumb for this 'overlength' is 1cm for each mm rope thickness, so 8cm for an 8mm rope. Milk the spare cover a few metres down the rope.

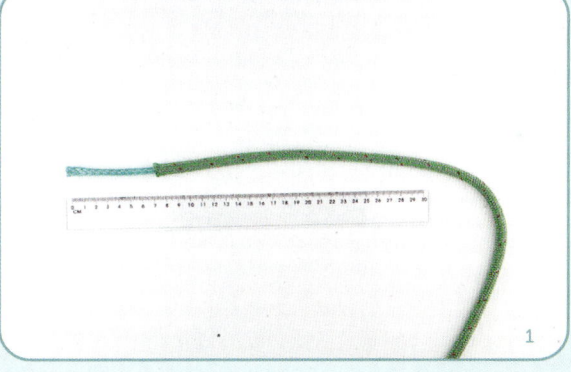

1

Take out the core from the cover at about 80cm from the tail end.

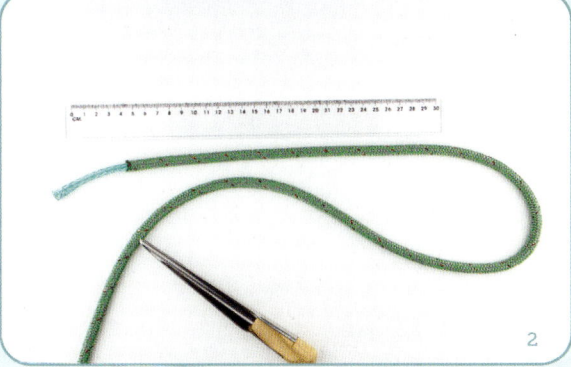

2

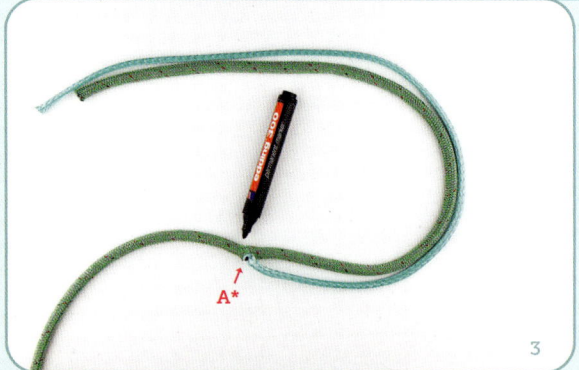

Mark point A* on the core at the point where it emerges from the cover.

Take the core further out from the cover and fix it temporarily in place with a needle.

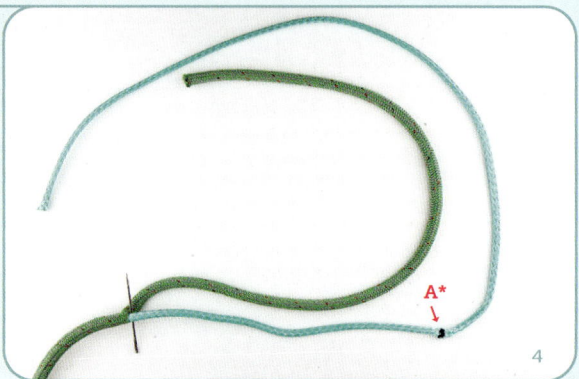

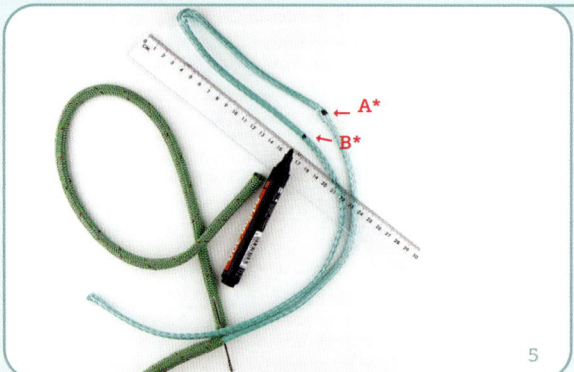

Determine the size of your soft shackle and mark point B* opposite point A*.

Place a fid in between A* and B* and lead the end of the core to A*.

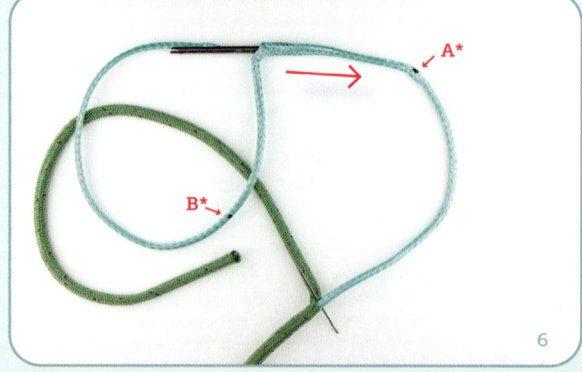

Put a round object through the loop and stretch the rope. Mark point C* on the inner rope at the intersection.

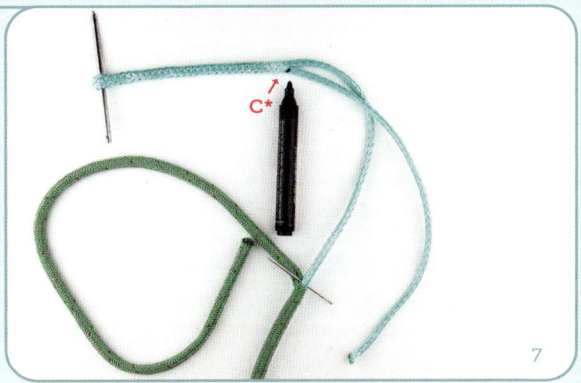

Insert the fid through the inner rope at C* and feed the long end of the whole rope through.

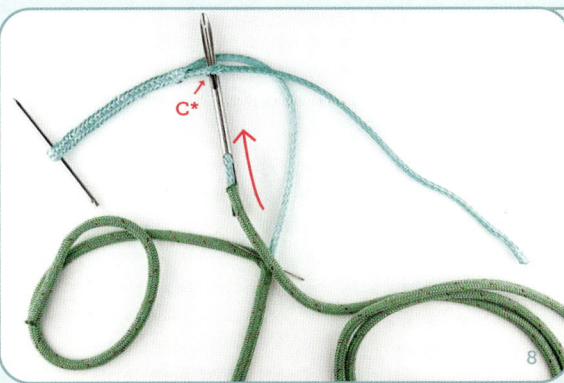

Pull the rope through fully. The loop is now locked.

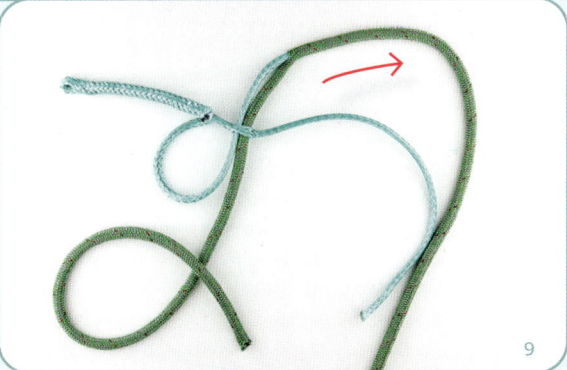

Take a single braid Dyneema line and thread the core through it.

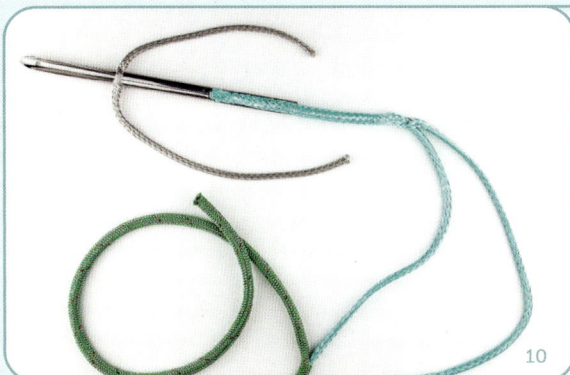

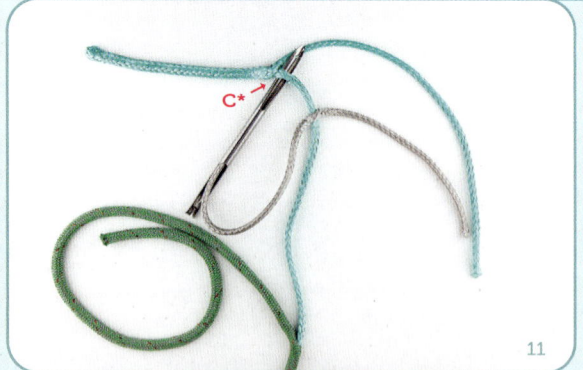

Fix the single braid Dyneema line in place at point C* by taking it through the inner rope first.

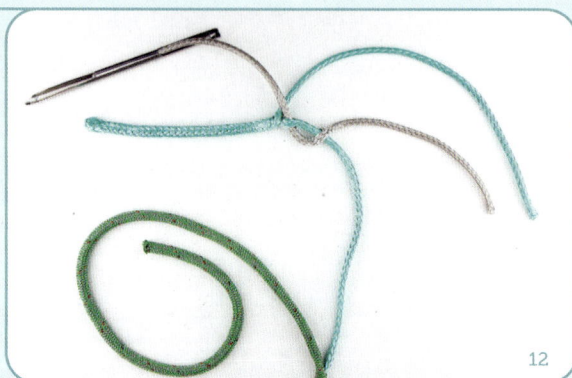

Pull the line through.

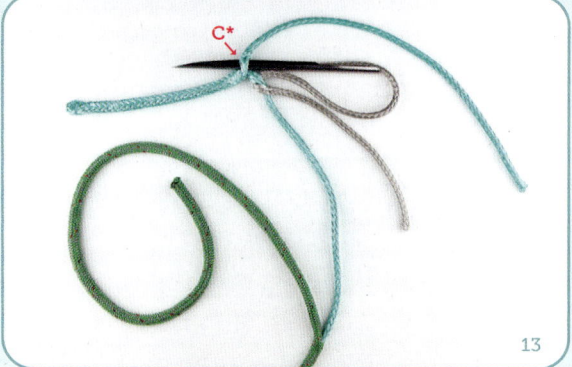

Now take the line through the outer rope at point C*.

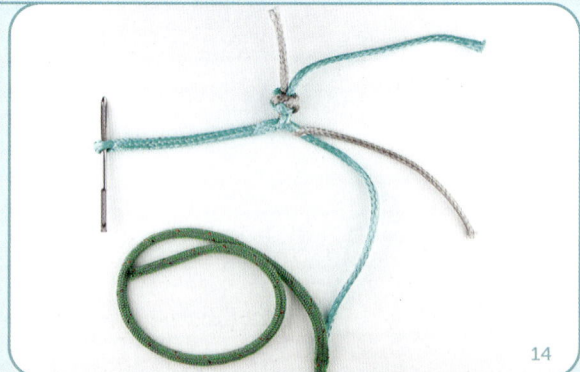

Tie a soft shackle knot with both ends, using the method on page 105.

Hide the single braid Dyneema line by taking it into the core with a pulling needle.

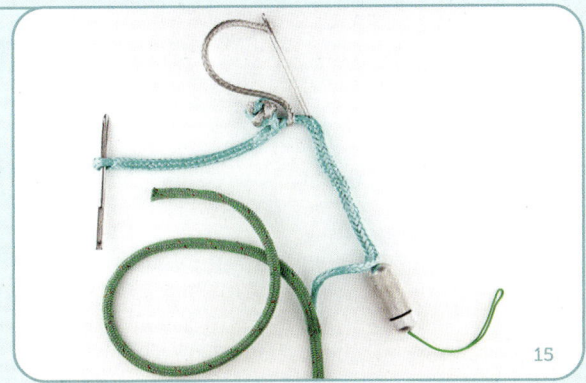

Taper the single braid Dyneema line and slide the core back over.

Make the eye of the soft shackle as large as possible. Take a thin line and feed it through the inner rope.

Feed the cover through the shackle and, with a pulling needle, tuck the cover about 5cm back into itself.

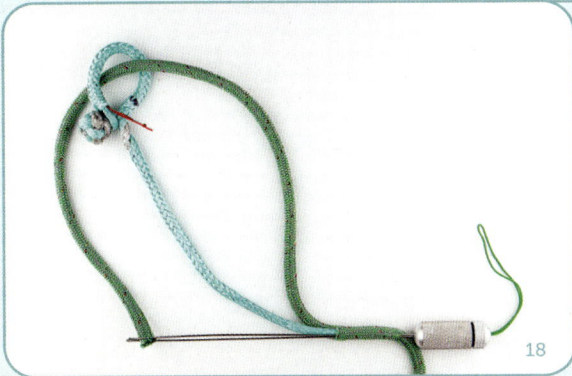

Milk the cover back up to the soft shackle.

19

Pull on the loop in the cover while milking the cover over.

20

21

To finish, pull on the end of the cover, cut it and stretch it again. Add a stitched whipping just below the eye.

This creates a Dyneema soft shackle integrated into a rope.

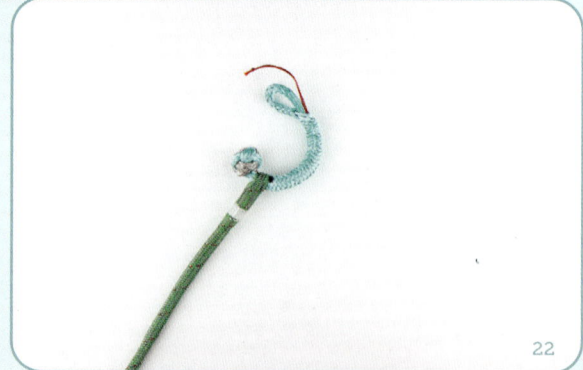

22

# Soft shackle knot

The so-called diamond knot is used as a stopper knot in soft shackles. The instructions below show this knot in detail

Use the two loose ends of the shackle. Make a loop in the red rope.

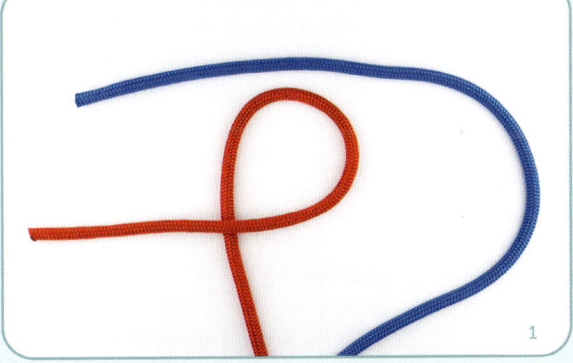

Start braiding. Lead the blue rope below the red rope, then over it and under it again.

Continue by leading the blue rope over itself and then below the red rope.

Pull the ends so that they are the same length.

Rotate the knot 180 degrees towards you.

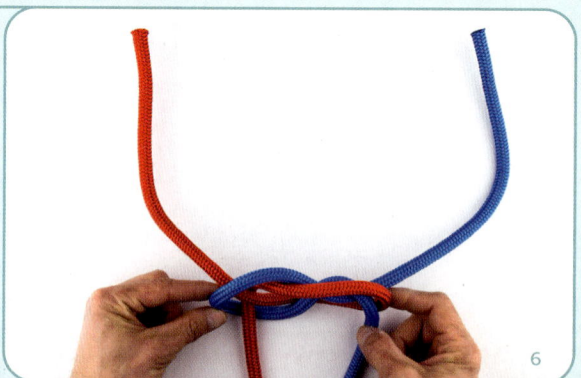

Take the red tail around the blue standing part and then lead it back up through the middle.

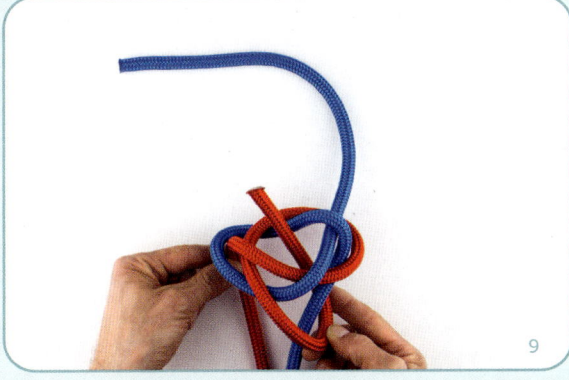

Repeat this with the blue tail: around the red standing part and up through the middle.

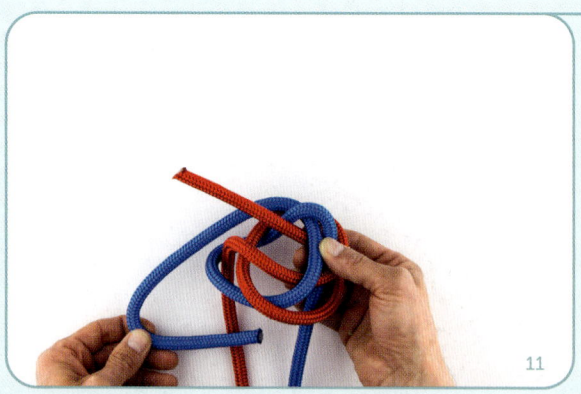

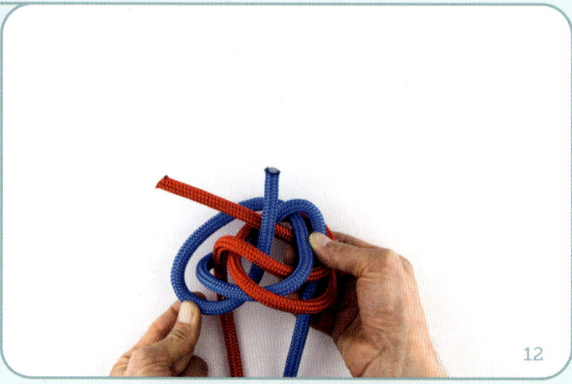

Pull both ends tightly and finish the soft shackle.

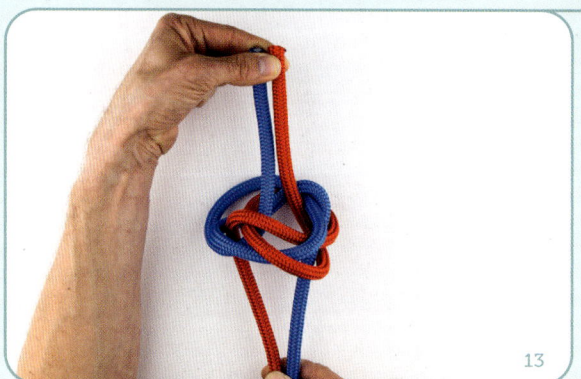

This creates a soft shackle knot.

# 9 Weight savings and tapering

You may want to taper a rope to save weight or to make it fit through a block or mast. There are several ways of doing this.

## Tapering a double braid Dyneema rope

To fill a spinnaker optimally in light weather, you can lighten the sheets by removing the cover in those parts where you don't need any grip. Use a rope with a coated Dyneema core. Because the core provides all the strength and you are not interfering with that, you don't have to worry about forces in this splice. The only aim is to have a smooth transition and cover finish.

Determine from where you want to taper the rope and take out the core from the cover at this point.

Spread the cover evenly over the core. Cut the cover so that you have about 35cm left.

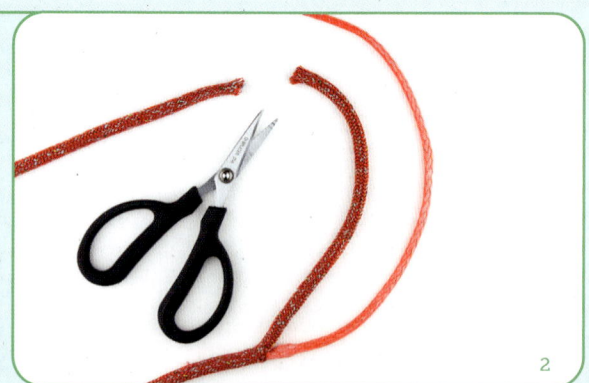

Insert a pulling needle into the core
about 45cm from junction and pull
the cover in to bury it completely.

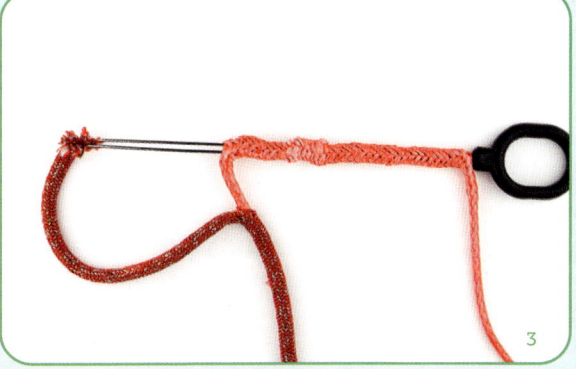

Secure the end of the cover with a
needle to prevent it from sliding in.
Tuck the core tightly over the cover
to create a smooth transition.

Add a stitched whipping (page 164)
to prevent the cover and core from
moving at point A.

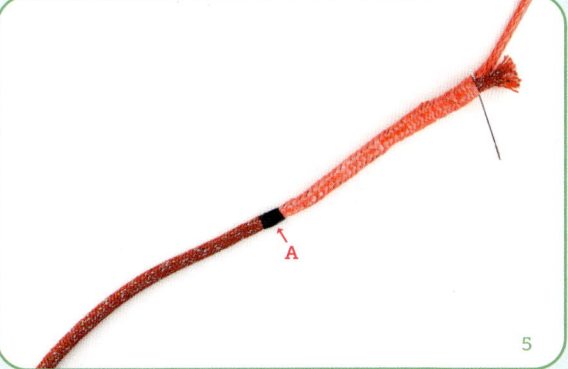

Taper the cover from about half the
distance to the whipping.

Slide the cover over the tapered cover.

7

This creates a tapered double braid Dyneema rope.

8

## Joining two single braid ropes

Another way to improve grip on a thin, strong Dyneema rope is to splice it to a hollow braid with grip fibre (such as Swiftcord).

Mark both ropes at 60 times the diameter of the thin rope (30cm for a 5mm rope).

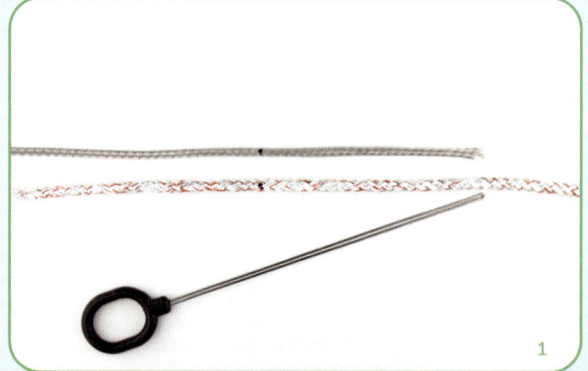

1

Insert a pulling needle into the thick rope at the correct distance along from the mark (about 35cm for a 5mm rope), and pull in the thin rope so that it can be buried completely.

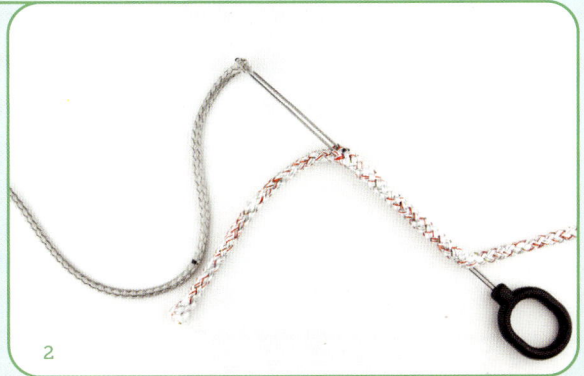

2

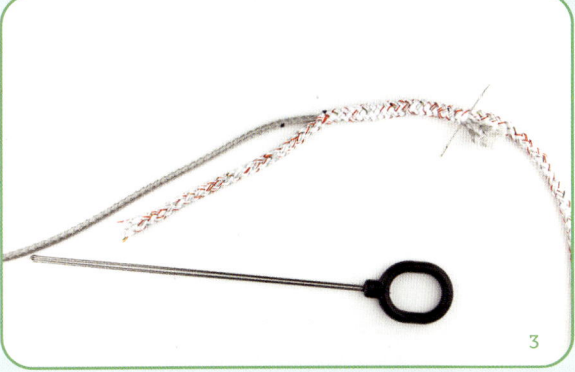

3

Secure the end of the rope using a needle. Insert the pulling needle into the thin rope about a third further than the length of the thick rope's tail.

Take the thick rope through the thin rope, and leave the tail sticking out. If the thin rope is a little tight, taper the gripline at this point (otherwise, do it in step 7).

4

5

Create a smooth transition by stretching the ropes.

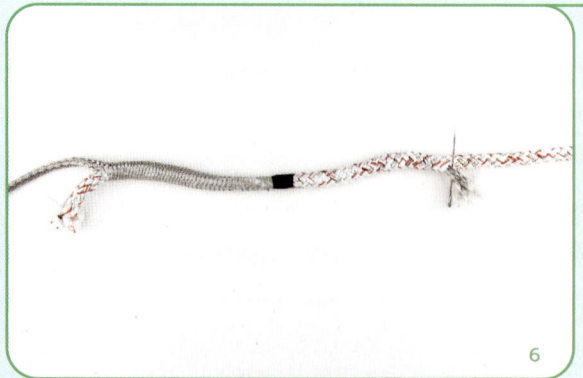

Add a stitched whipping.

6

Taper both ends (if you haven't already done so during step 4).

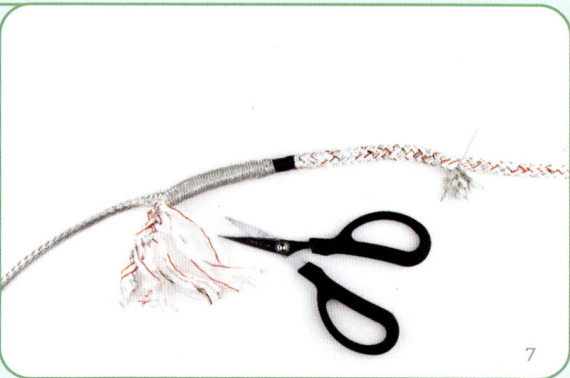

7

Slide the ropes over each other on both sides.

8

This creates two single braid ropes spliced together.

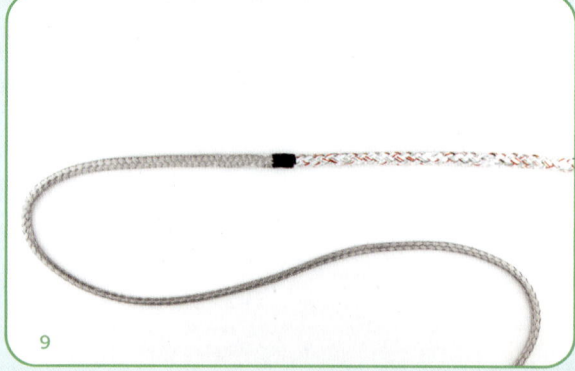

9

# Joining steel wire with double braid polyester

Some boats still have a steel wire lead for their polyester halyard. This method is old-fashioned but effective; minimal stretch is combined with the decent grip of a polyester rope. You could replace the steel wire lead with a thin Dyneema rope, as is shown on page 121. If the sheave in the masthead is one that can hold a rope, you can simply use a double braid Dyneema rope.

In some situations there is no alternative to the steel wire lead. In this case, use a flexible 7x19 steel wire – this has seven strands of 19 wire threads; one goes through the core with the other six laid around it. That makes this splice quite similar to the splice of a three-strand laid rope (see page 22).

You can also use a single braid rope, in which case you can skip steps 16–19.

This splice can be slightly complicated because it is hard to get the fid into the rigid steel wire.

Tape the wire at about 50cm from the end (A), and divide the tail end into six by marking it five times as shown.

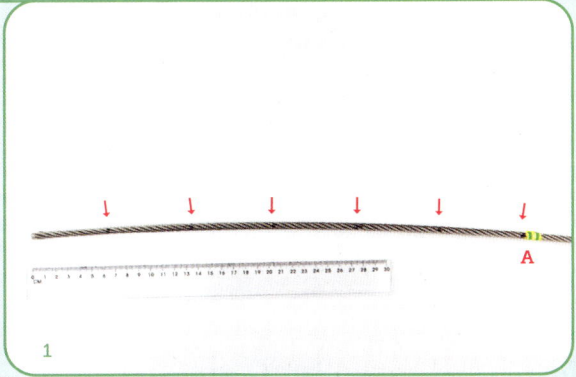

1

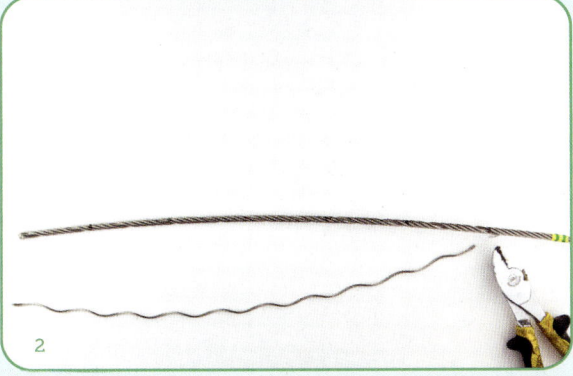

2

Unlay one of the strands as far as the last marker, close to point A, and cut it with a wire cutter. It is important to use a sharp wire cutter to avoid getting loose threads.

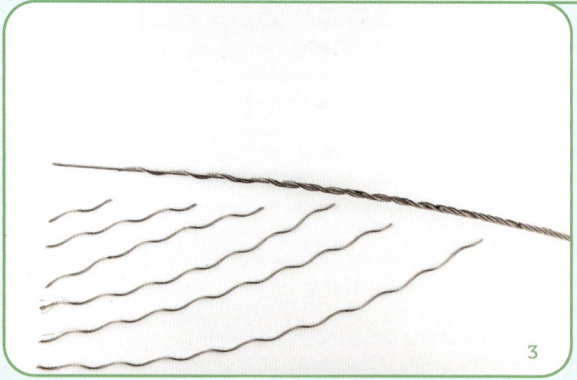

Repeat this for the other five strands so that the steel wire is tapered systematically.

Cover the tapered part of the steel wire with tape.

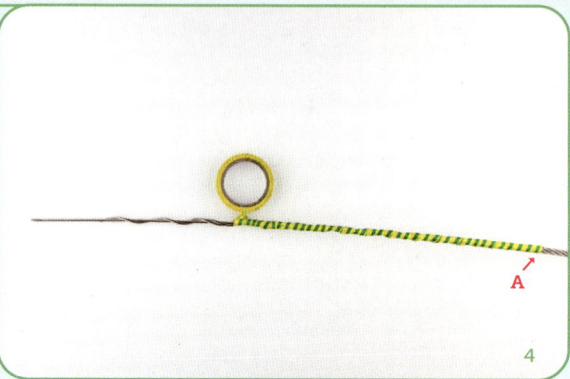

Pull out about 25cm of the core from the polyester rope and tape the end before you cut it.

Pull a further 80cm of the core from the cover and fix it in place with a fid. Fix a small fid to the steel wire.

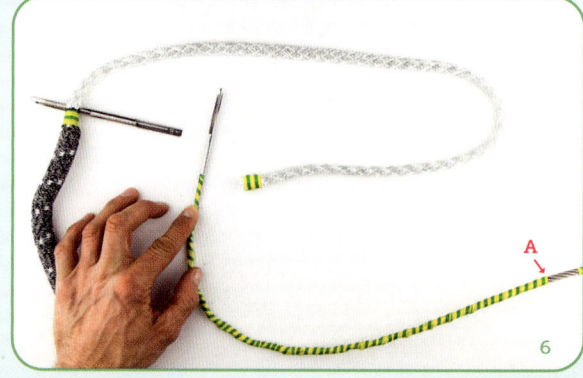

Feed the steel wire into the core.

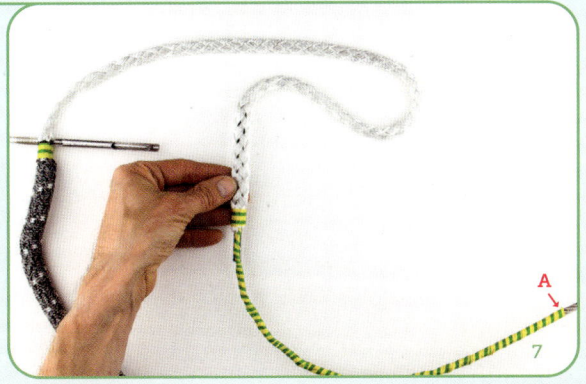

Pull out the steel wire when point A
has gone about 20cm into the core.

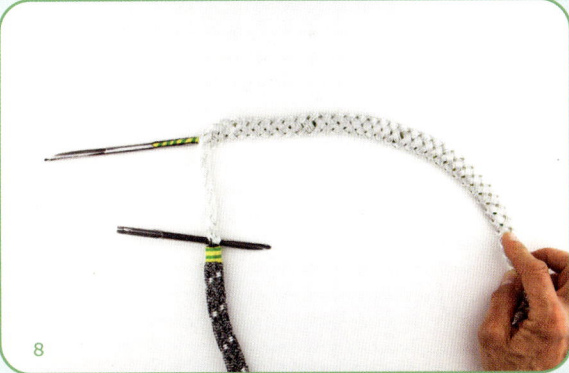

Tape the core at point A.

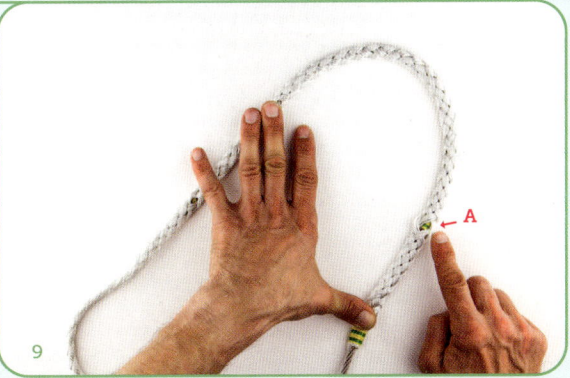

Unlay the core up to the tape at
point A.

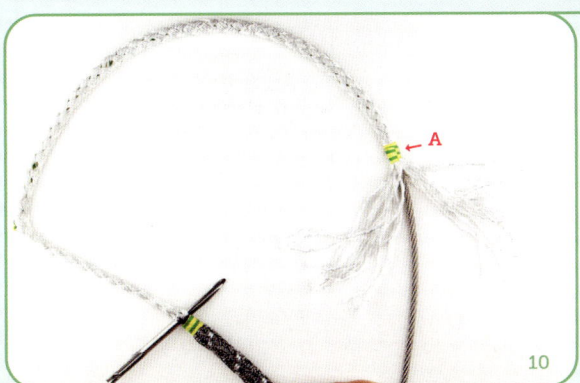

117

Divide the core into three equal bundles and tape them as shown. Insert the fid under two strands of the wire against the direction of the lay.

Pull one bundle of the core below the two strands of the steel wire and tighten.

At the point where the core bundle emerges, insert the fid again under the next two wire strands. Do the same for the last bundle.

When all three core bundles have been fed under the two steel wire strands, repeat the previous steps at least twice more.

All bundles have been braided through the steel wire at least three times now. Cut or melt the ends back to the steel wire.

15

16

Take the cover back over the transition with the steel wire. Make sure the cover is well stretched.

Determine the end of the steel wire transition and tape the rope just below that point.

17

18

Pull out the cover and divide it into three equal bundles. Repeat steps 11–15.

Melt the strands when they have been braided through the steel wire at least three times.

19

If you like, wrap whipping twine around the transition.

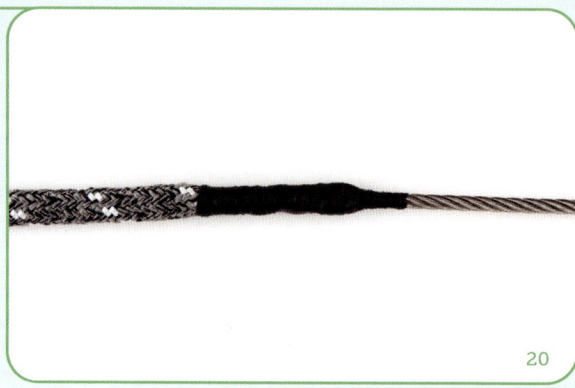

20

This creates a steel wire lead connected to double braid polyester.

21

# Joining a single braid Dyneema rope with double braid polyester

If you don't have enough space in the mast for a thicker halyard, use single braid Dyneema instead of steel wire (see page 115) because it is lighter. If you have a double braid Dyneema halyard, you have to taper it as on page 110.

Use a loosely braided Dyneema rope as a lead so that you have enough space to splice both the polyester core and the cover to it.

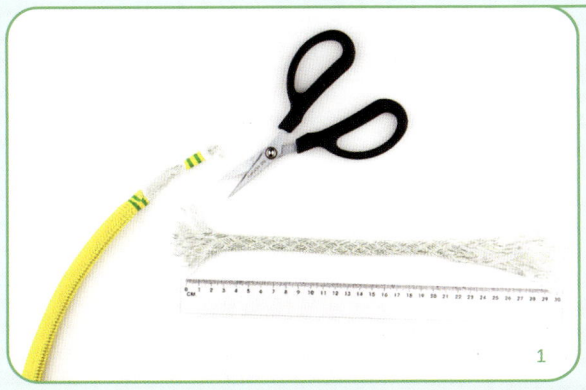

Take the core from the polyester rope and tape it at 75 times the diameter of the Dyneema lead (about 30cm for a 4mm lead). Cut the core.

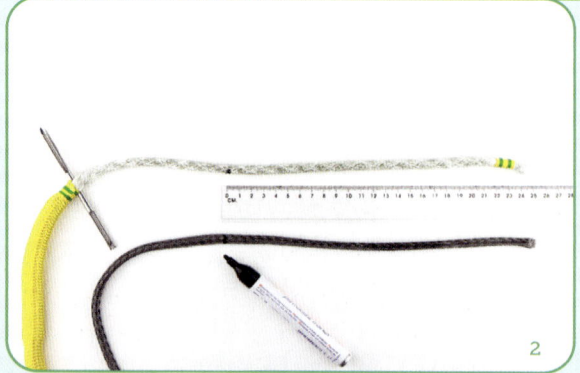

Pull the core further from the cover and secure it with a needle. Mark a point 60 times the lead diameter on both ropes (24cm for a 4mm lead).

Pull the polyester core through the Dyneema rope until the marks on both ropes meet.

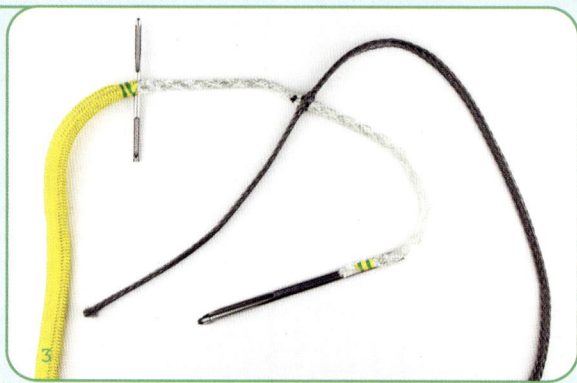

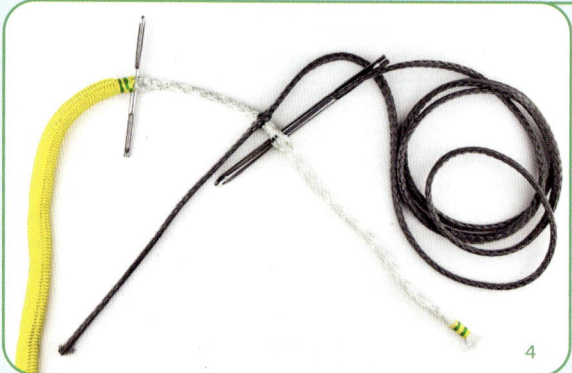

Pull the Dyneema rope slightly to one side, to place a fid right through the polyester core at the mark. Feed the longer end of the lead through the core.

The splice is now locked.

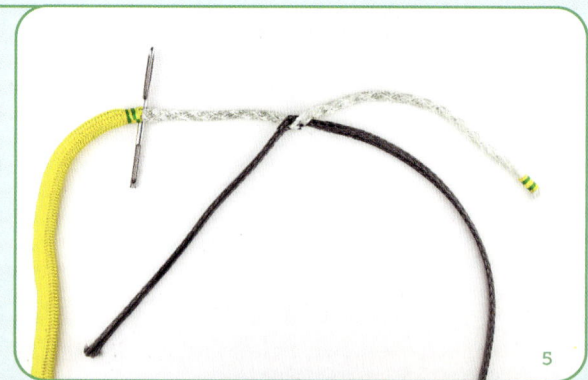

122

Take the shorter end of the Dyneema lead into the polyester core.

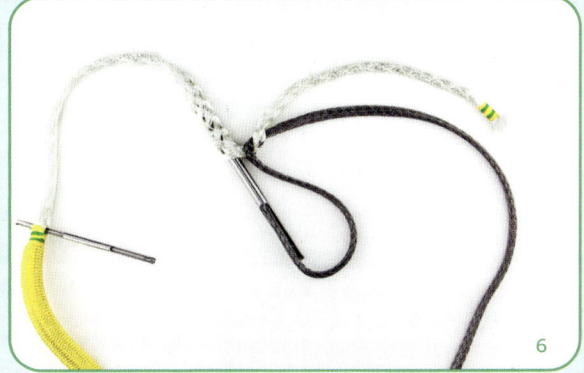

6

7

Taper the Dyneema lead by cutting it diagonally and milk the polyester core over the tapered Dyneema lead.

Take the polyester core into the Dyneema lead. Use a pulling needle (or soft fid – see page 176) if there is limited space in the core.

8

9

Take out the needle at such a distance that the polyester core can be completely buried inside the Dyneema lead.

Taper the polyester core.

10

Slide the Dyneema lead over the polyester core. The core is now spliced into the Dyneema rope.

11

12

Slide the cover back over the junction of the core with the Dyneema lead. Make sure the cover is completely stretched out.

Mark the cover at 60 times the lead diameter (24cm for a 4mm lead).

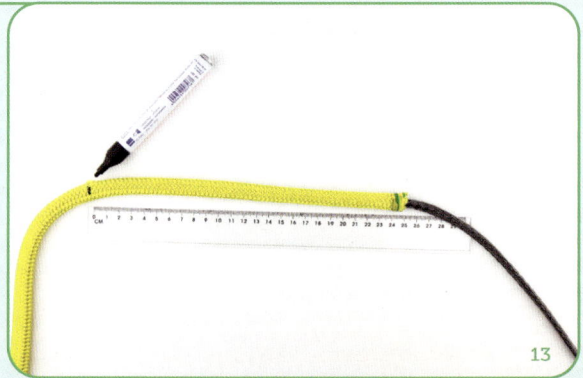

13

Pull out the Dyneema lead completely at the mark on the polyester cover.

Mark the Dyneema lead at the point where it emerged from the cover. Always make sure that the polyester cover is stretched out and not riding up anywhere.

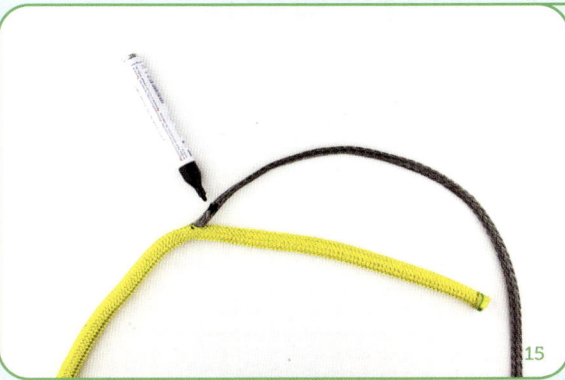

At the mark on the lead, take the polyester cover into the Dyneema lead. Use a pulling needle (or soft fid – see page 176) if there is limited space

Have a needle emerge at such a distance that the polyester cover can be completely buried inside the Dyneema lead.

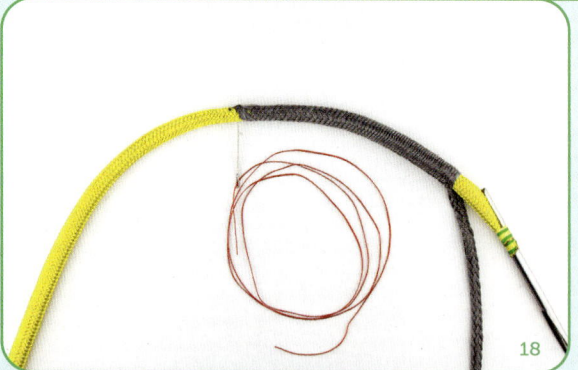

Add a stitched whipping on the transition of cover and lead.

Taper the polyester cover.

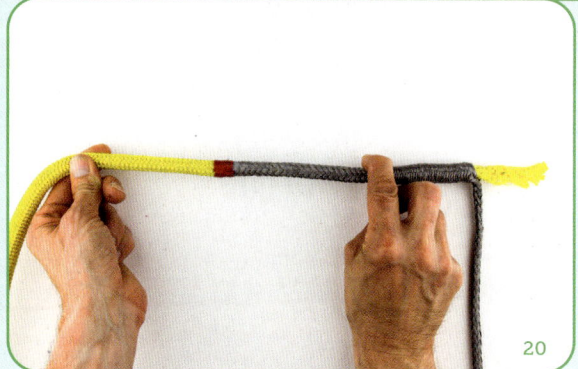

Slide the Dyneema lead over the polyester cover.

This creates a single braid Dyneema lead joined to double braid polyester.

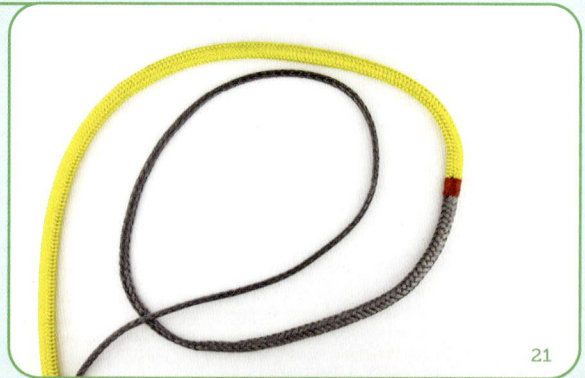

# 10 Thickening and strengthening

When ropes slip in a clutch, you can thicken them locally by splicing an extra cover or core into them. To thicken a rope for a clutch, use a polyester cover or a mix with an aramid fibre (more wear resistant); a cover of pure Dyneema would be too slippery.

An extra cover can also be used to protect a rope from wear at critical points; use a Dyneema cover for this because it is very durable. One example is the point at which the spinnaker halyard moves back and forth through the sheave or block at the masthead.

## Splicing in an extra cover

Feed the rope through the extra cover with a fid. Leave some spare room on each side.

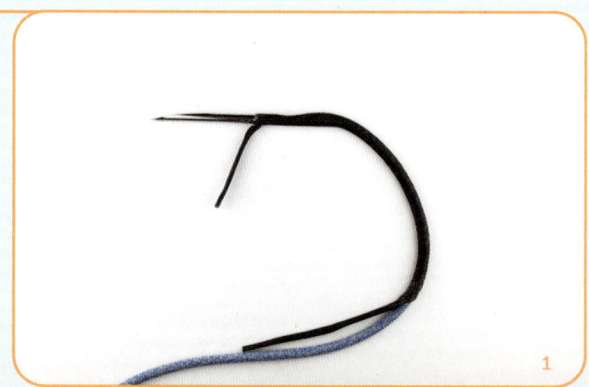

1

Make the cover over the area you want to thicken or protect.

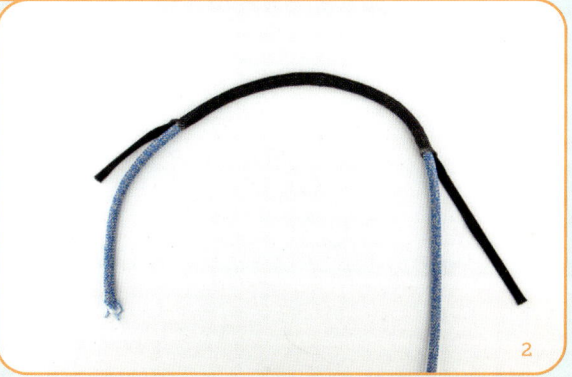

Pull the extra cover through the rope cover with a pulling needle so that it can be buried completely. You can also use a soft fid (see page 176) if there is limited space in the rope. Instead of pulling the full cover in the rope you can also unlay the cover, divide it into 3 bundles and pull 3 bundles in the rope.

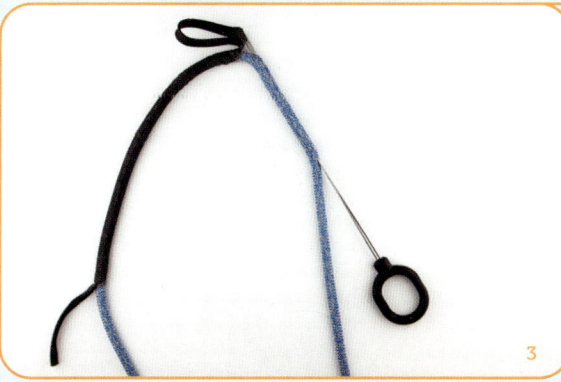

Add a stitched whipping over the transition. Cut the end of the extra cover diagonally.

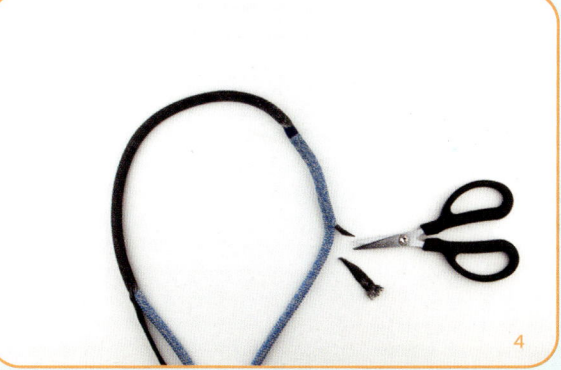

Slide the rope back. Repeat the previous steps on the other side.

This creates a rope with an extra cover spliced in.

6

## Sewing in an extra cover

If you'd like a smoother transition, sew in the extra cover. This is also useful where the rope is braided very tightly. Although it is not very difficult, it is a lot of work.

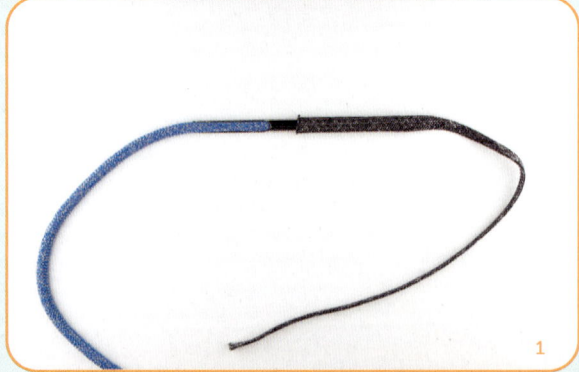

Feed the rope through the extra cover with a fid.

1

Slide the cover over the area you want to thicken or protect.

2

Tape the extra cover about 15–20cm from its tail.

3

Unlay the extra cover.

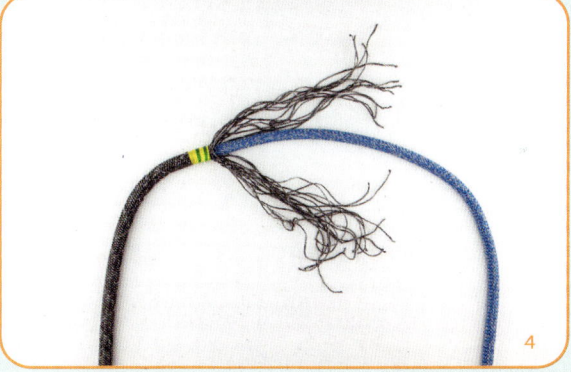

4

One by one, sew the strands through the rope using a zigzag stitch.

5

Ensure an even spread by varying where you finish stitching the strands.

This creates a rope with an extra cover sewn in.

## Strip and recover

For halyards and sheets with a Dyneema core you can replace the cover of the last part of the rope with a thin abrasion resistant Dyneema cover. This has several advantages. The Dyneema cover makes the last part of the rope extra abrasion resistant. The splice with the thin Dyneema cover at the end is thinner and more flexible than a splice with the original (thicker) cover. This technique is particularly popular with racing boats and combines several techniques from this book.

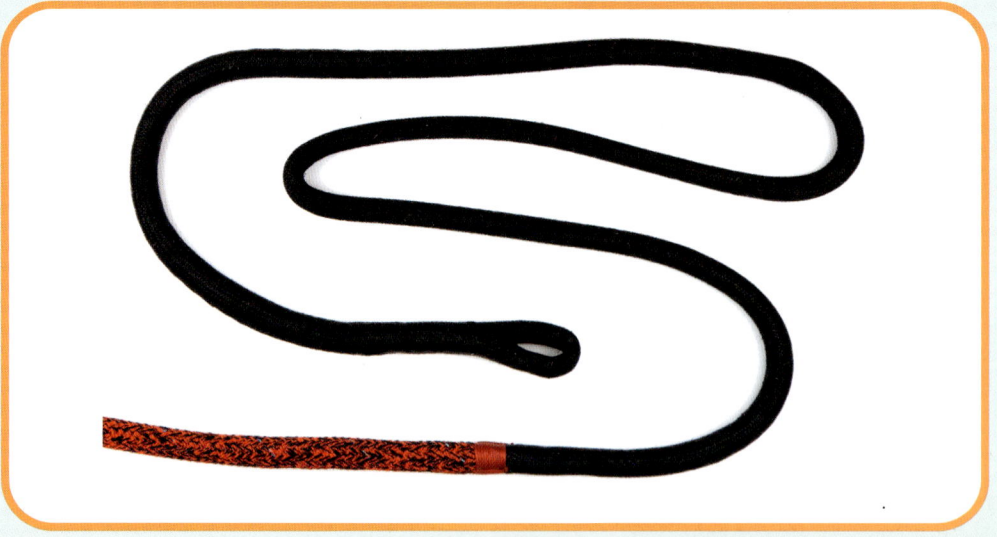

Taper the rope over 2.5m as explained in chapter 9 (page 110). Instead of a whipping, use a few stitches to fix the cover to the core.

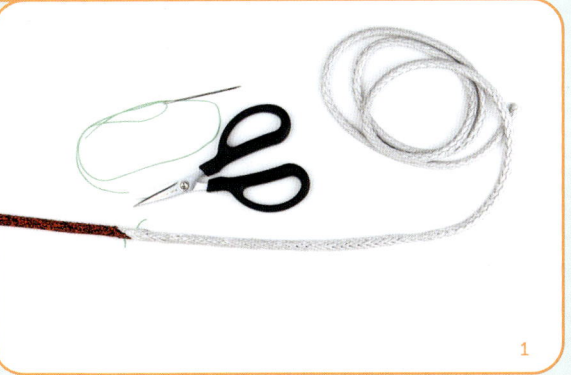

Feed the rope through the Dyneema cover with a fid.

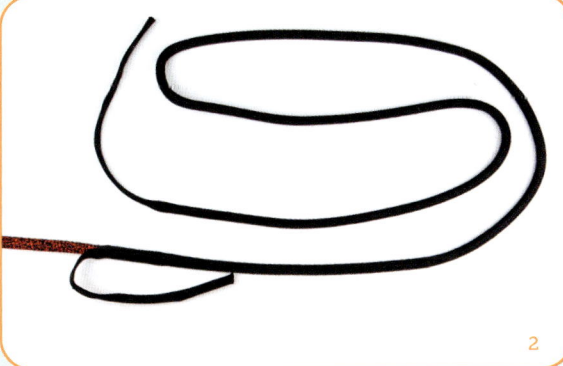

Make a covered eye splice as explained in chapter 7 (page 78).

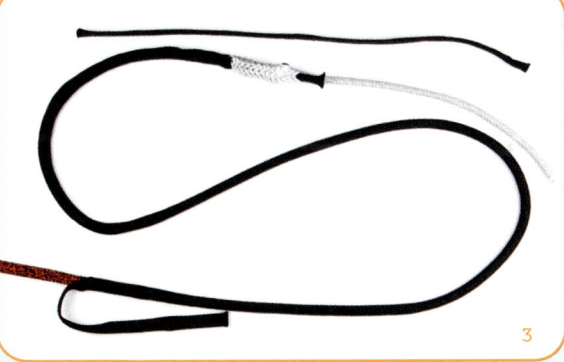

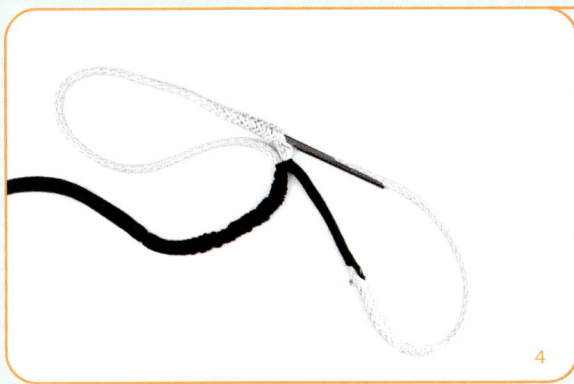

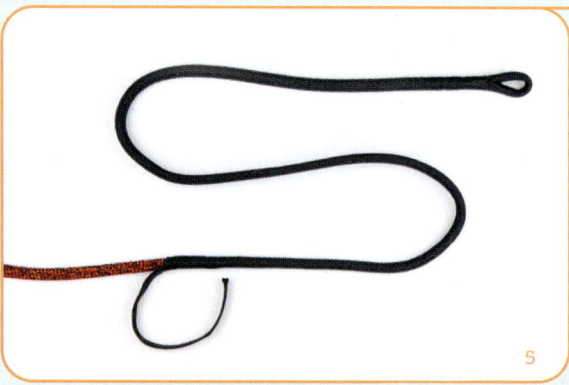

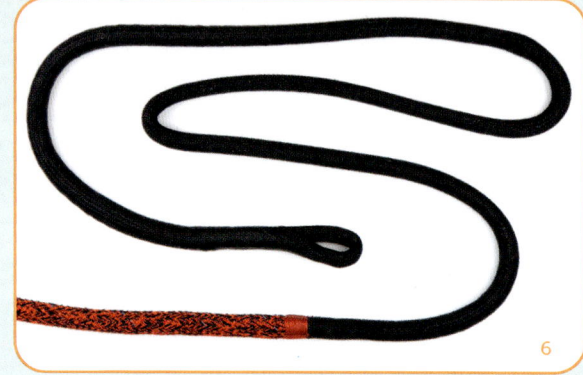

Milk the cover. Pull the cover into the rope and finish with a whipping, as explained in the previous paragraphs.

## Splicing in an extra core

If your rope won't hold in your clutch, or if you want to thicken it for any other reason, you can splice in an extra core. It is recommended to use the same material for both the core of the rope and the extra core.

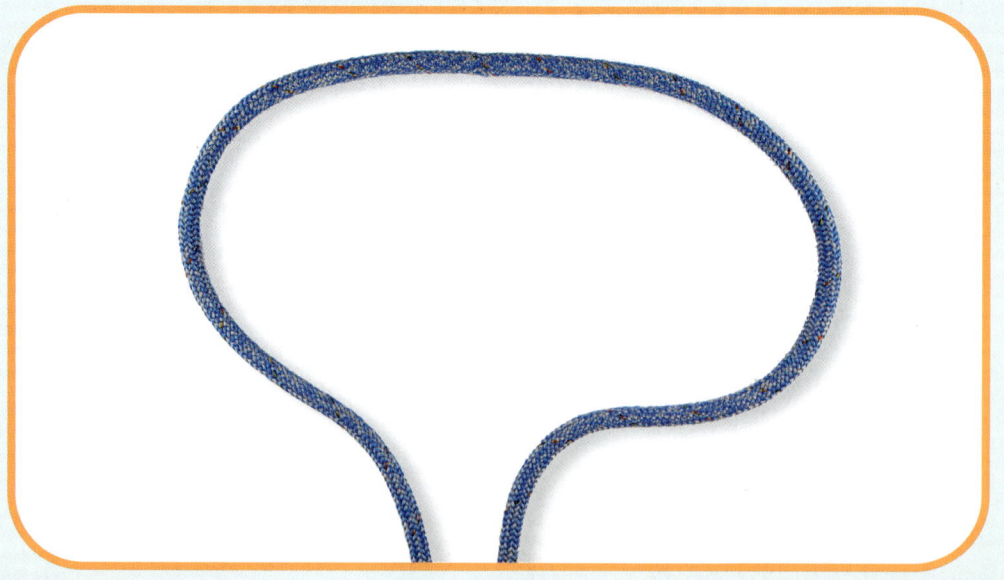

Take the core from the cover at the point from where you want to splice in the extra core.

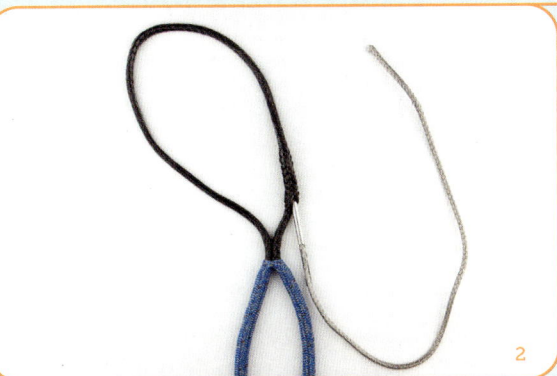

Pull the extra core into the rope core with a fid or a pulling needle, depending on the length.

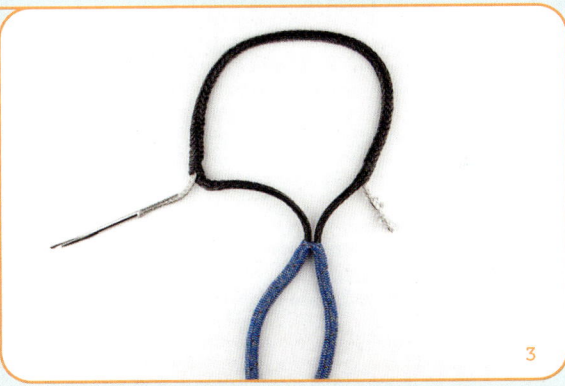

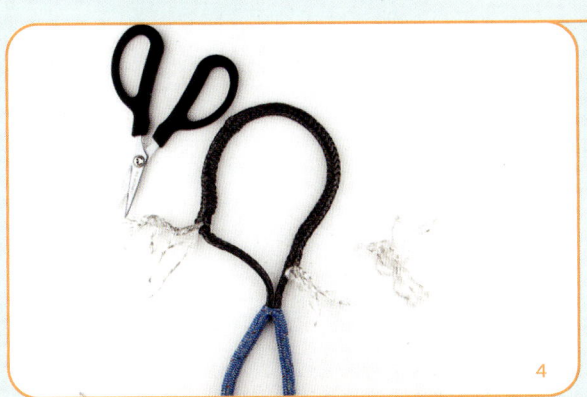

Taper the ends of the extra core.

Milk the core back from the centre.

Milk the cover back over the thickened core.

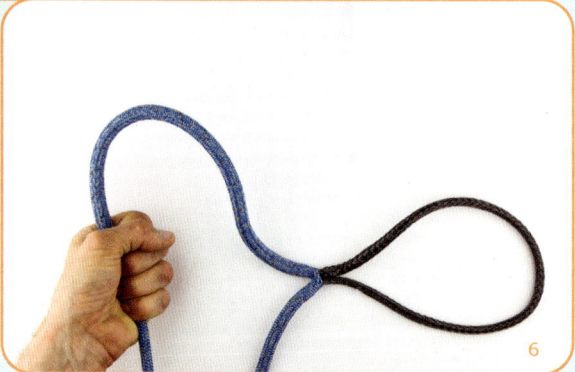

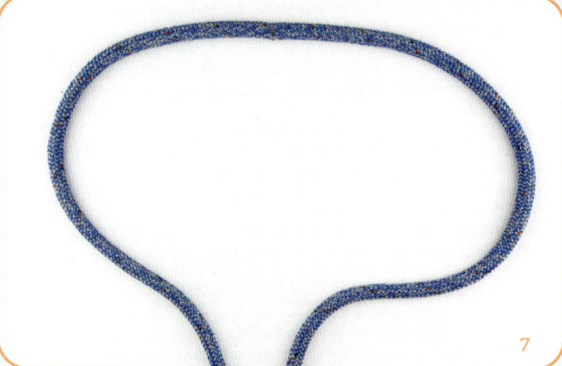

This creates a rope with an extra core spliced in.

# 11 Continuous loops

## Double braid polyester

Continuous ropes are often used for sheets and in furlers. Their even thickness makes them move smoothly through the blocks. About 70% of the strength of a polyester rope comes from its core and 30% from its cover. It is therefore important to splice both core and cover to maintain strength.

Two methods are explained below. The first option produces a perfectly even rope in terms of thickness, but is less strong because the core isn't spliced to itself. The second method incorporates that (see page 142) so the rope is a lot stronger, but the diameter will be thicker in the spliced area.

## For equal thickness, spliced without the core

This method provides a weaker rope than the one on page 142. In most cases you won't need this strength, so this easier splice will do. It is, for example, commonly used in roller furling systems.

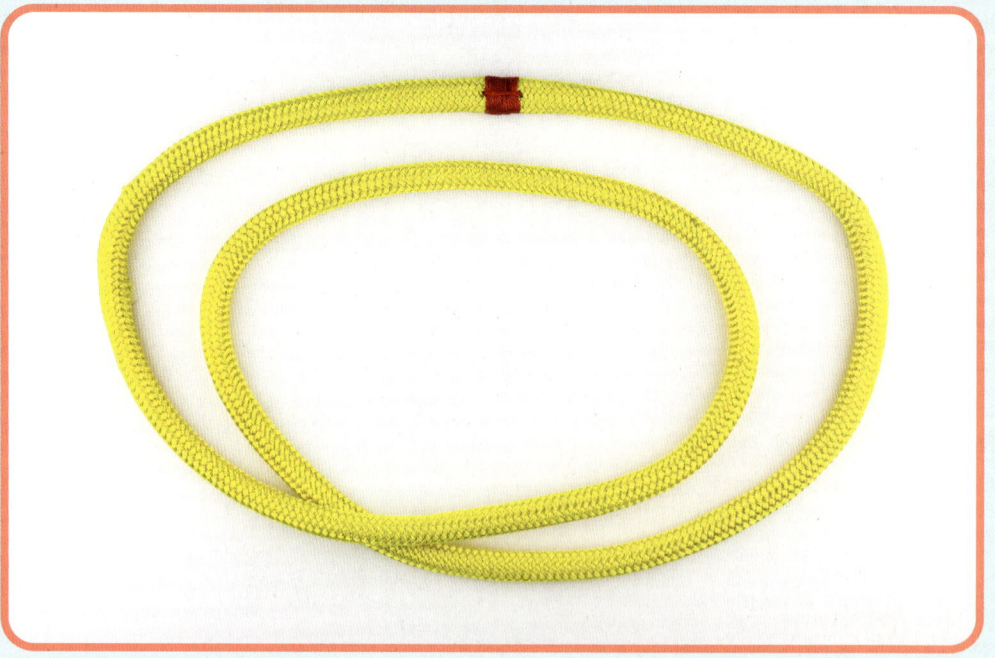

Mark points A1, A2, B1, B2. Use a fid with a similar thickness to the rope diameter.

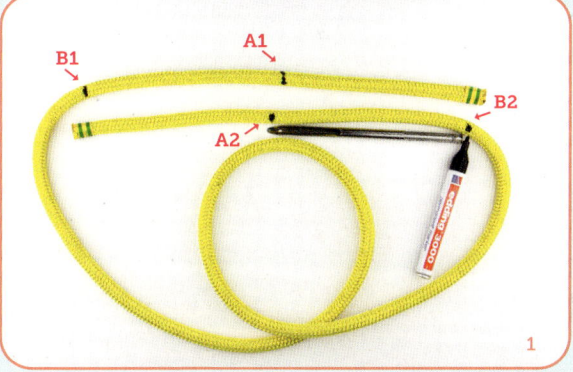

Take the core from the cover at B1 and B2.

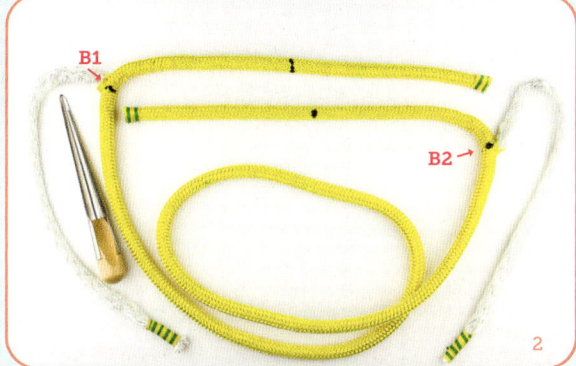

Insert the fid into the cover at A2. Take the cover from the other end and tape it to the fid. Use a pulling needle (or soft fid – see page 176) if there is limited space.

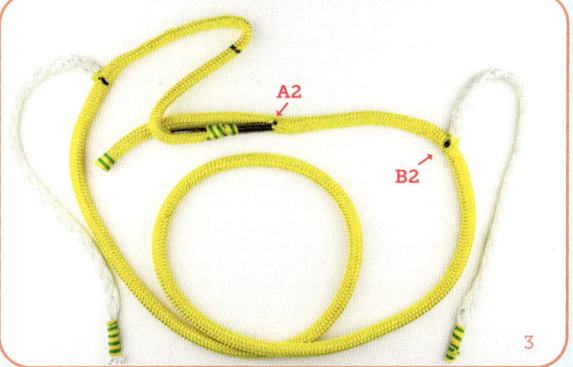

Pull out the fid and cover a few centimetres past B2.

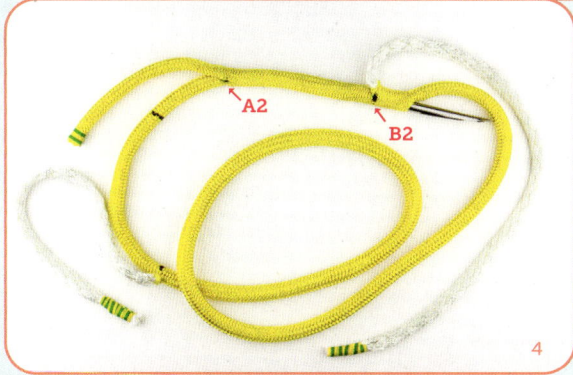

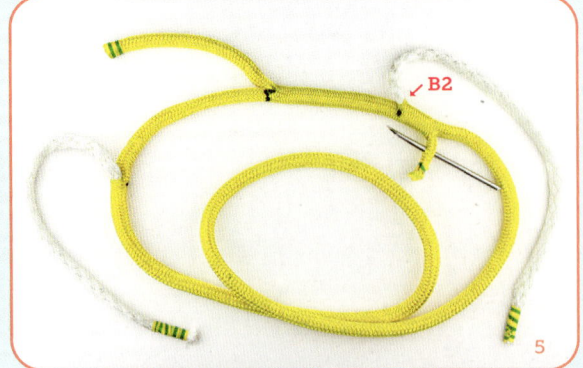

At point B2, secure the cover in place with a fid.

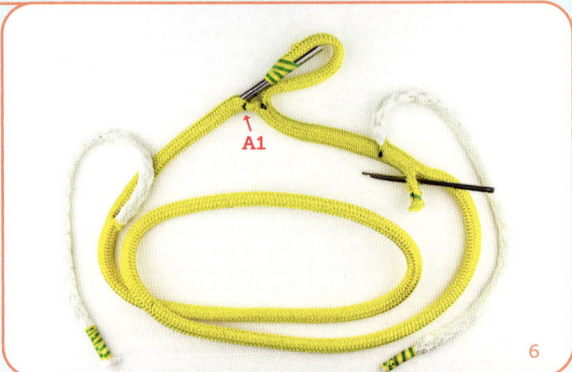

Insert the fid into the cover at point A1.

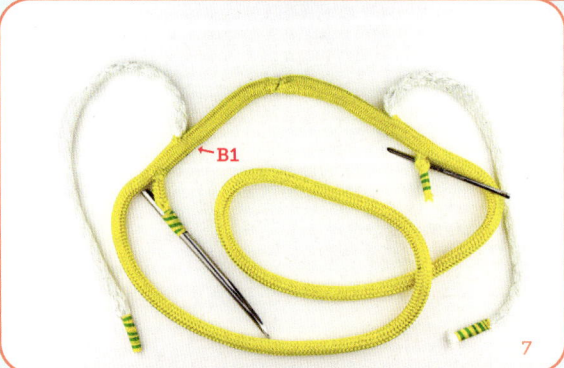

Pull out the fid and cover a few centimetres past B1.

Tuck the cover back into the rope from the centre. Put some tension on the rope so that you can evenly distribute the cover and core around the loop. Make sure the cover it not riding up anywhere.

Mark the points at which the core emerges from the cover on both sides.

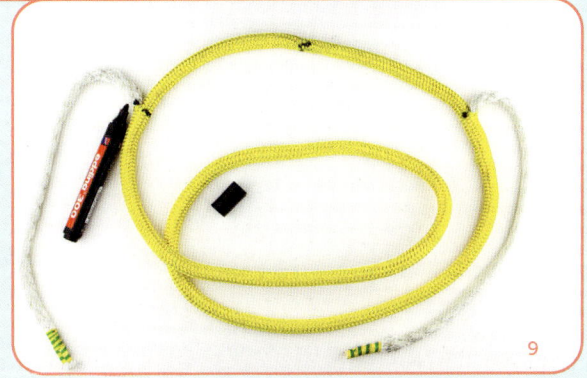

Try to feel the amount of overlap in the core and take this amount of core from the cover. This should be a few centimetres from the marks. Cut the core at this point to create a smooth transition. Repeat this for the other side.

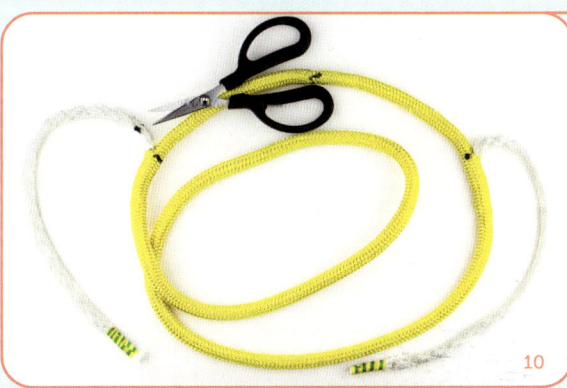

Tuck the core back into the cover.

Add a stitched whipping over the transition of cores and covers.

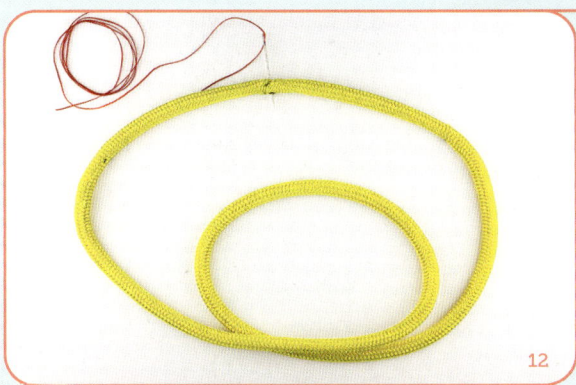

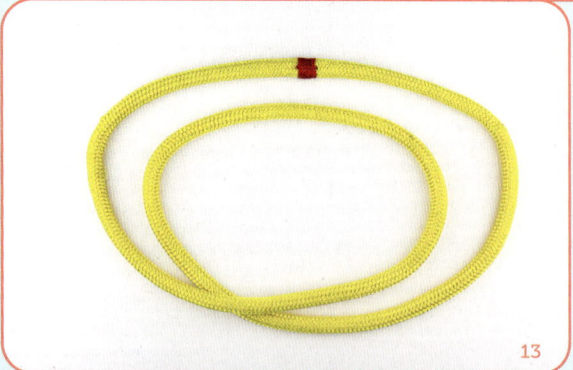

This creates continuous ropes of double braid polyester with an even thickness.

## For strength, spliced with the core

If you want to maintain the full strength of the rope, you need to incorporate the core in the splice as shown below. It makes the spliced area thicker. This splice is mainly used for sheets with no or negligible purchase (also called German sheeting) and for mooring lines.

If you want the spliced area to be thinner, taper both cores after step 7, while maintaining its structure (see page 20), and repeat this for both covers at step 19.

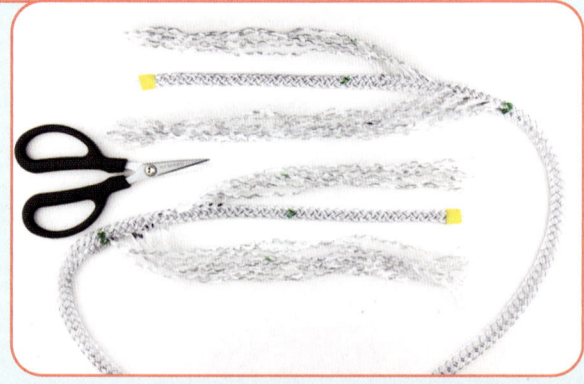

Tie two knots at about 2 metres from the ends. Create some room in the rope by cutting out 10–15cm of core on each side. Tape the ends.

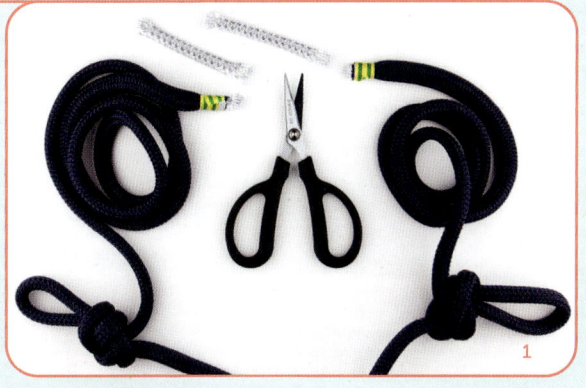

Keep the core and cover together at the tail end and tuck up the spare cover towards the knot. Repeat on the other side.

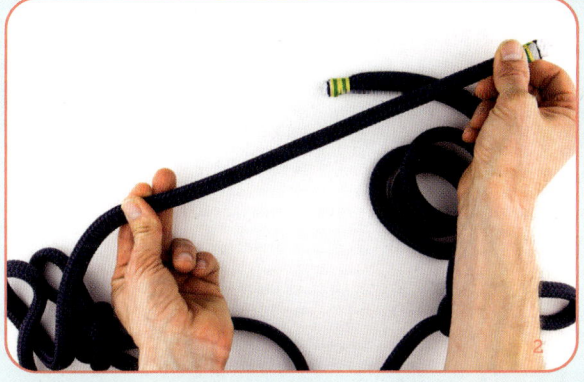

Pull the core from the cover at three times the fid length and mark each fid length on the core (A1, B1, C1).

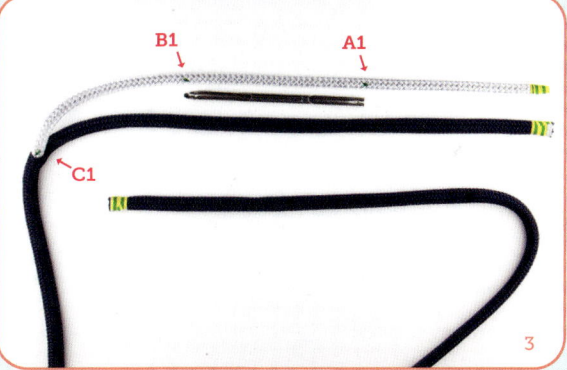

Repeat on the other side (A2, B2, C2).

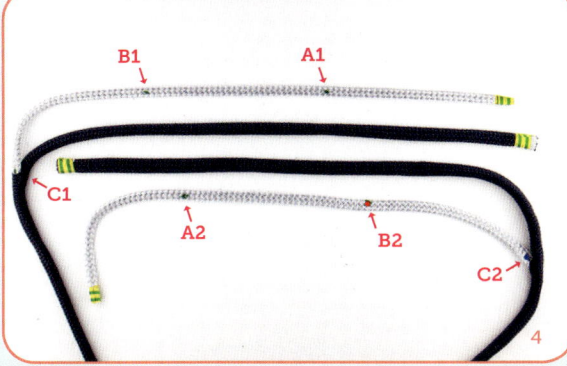

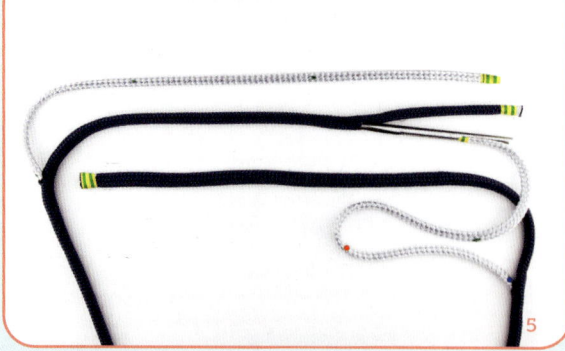

Insert the fid in the cover at one fid length and pull through the core from the other side.

5

Take out the fid with the core at the point where the second core emerges from the cover

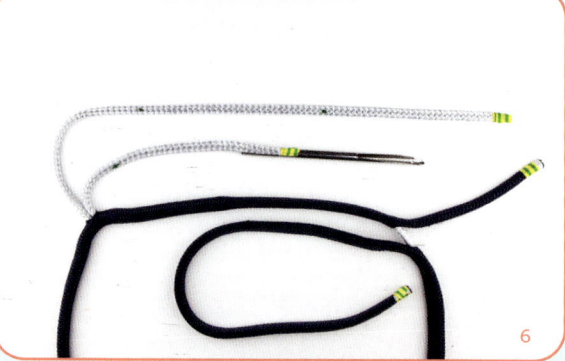

6

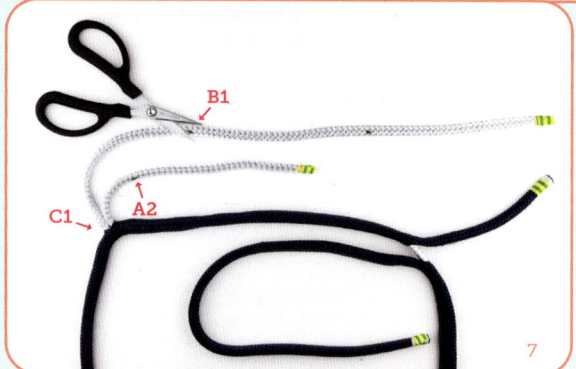

B1

C1 → A2

7

Cut the second core (which has not passed through the cover) at twice the fid length (B1).

Take the first, uncut core through the second core at C1.

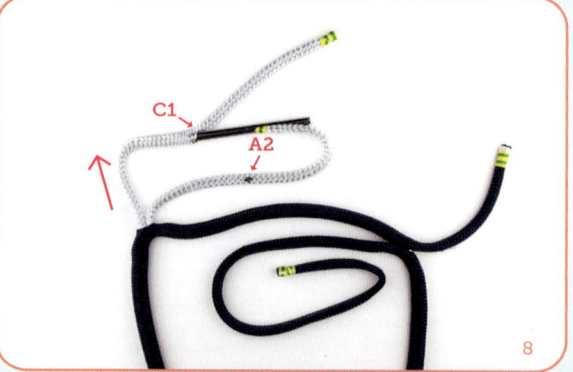

C1

A2

8

Pull out the fid at such a distance that the core can be completely buried inside up to point A2 (one fid length).

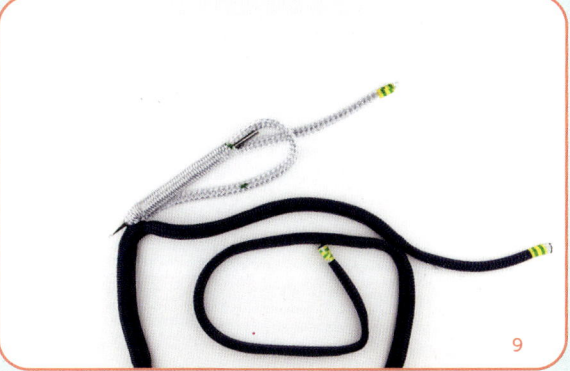

9

Secure the end of the first core with a needle. Insert a fid into the core at A2.

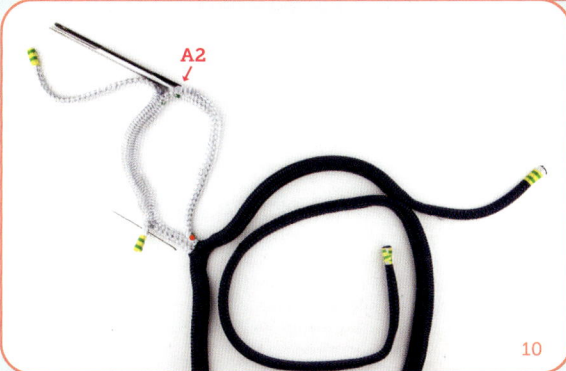

10

Take out the fid at such a distance that one core can be completely buried inside the other.

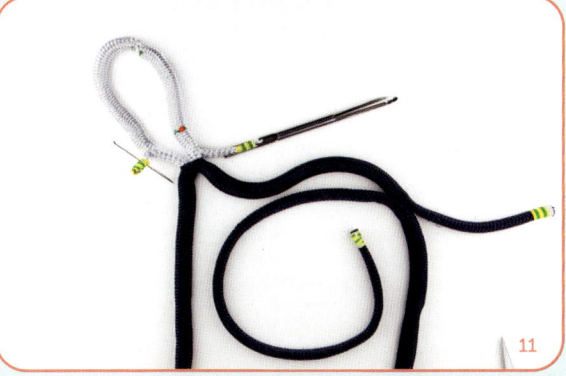

11

Taper the core at both ends.

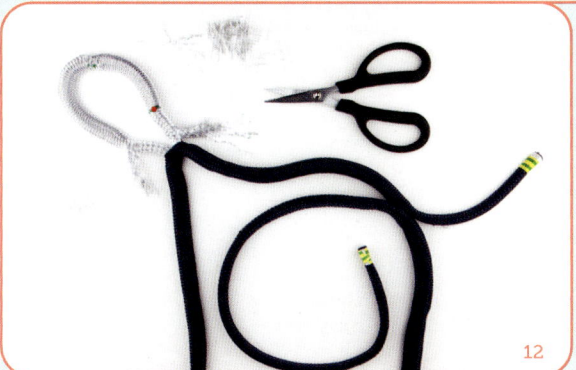

12

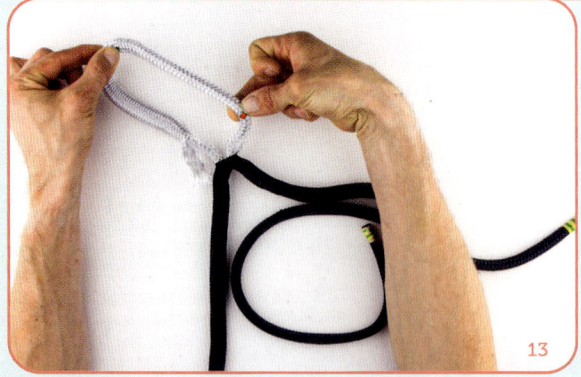

Pull the core from the centre over the splices.

Secure the transition with a few stitches so that it won't slip.

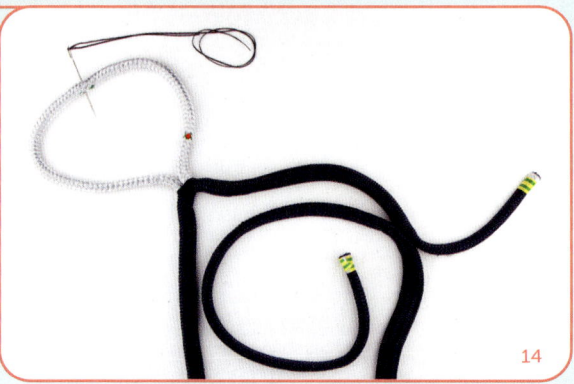

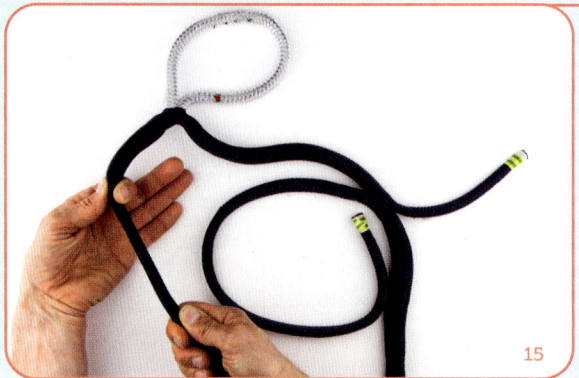

The cores are now spliced together and can be tucked back into the cover.

Milk the cover over the core at both ends.

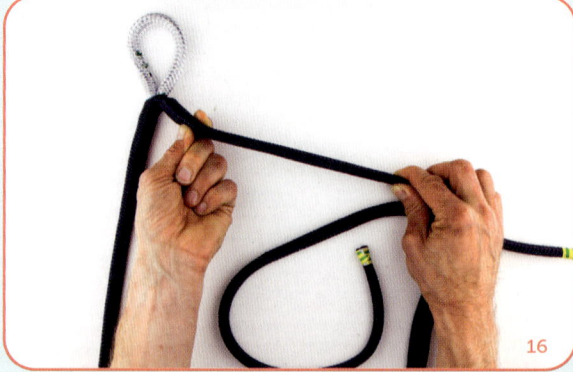

Take out the core at the point where the two covers meet.

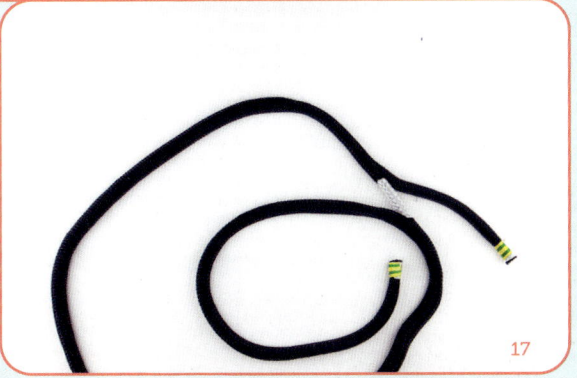

17

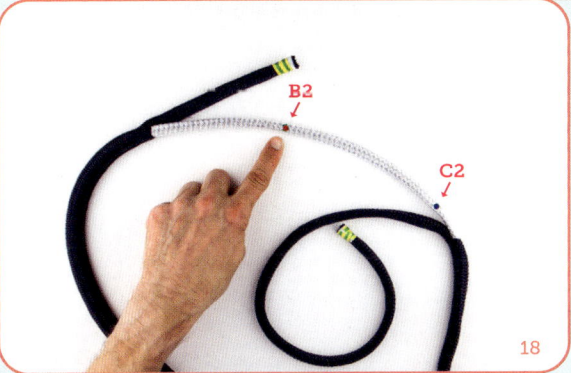

18

Now that point B2 has emerged, this is where the core transition ends. The cover transition will be made between B2 and C2.

Take the cover from the second end through the core from C2 to B2 as shown.

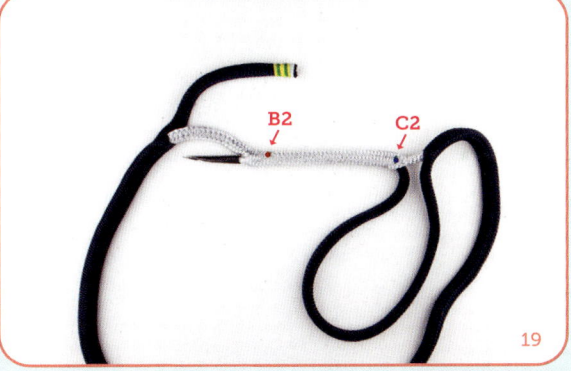

19

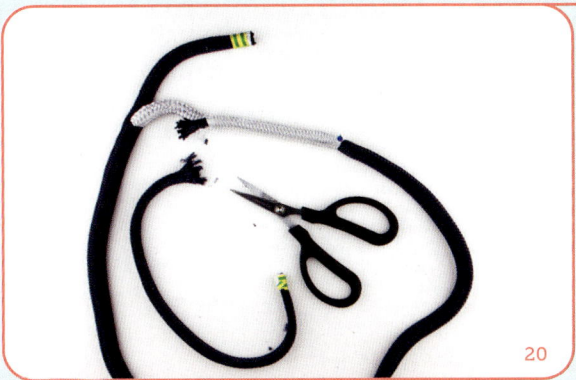

20

Cut the cover diagonally so that you can bury it inside the core.

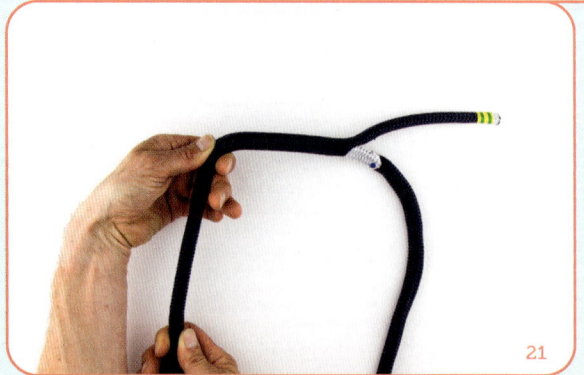

Milk the loose cover (the one that hasn't gone through the core) over the core. Make sure the cover is stretched out through the loop.

Insert the pulling needle far enough into the cover so that the loose cover can be completely buried inside.

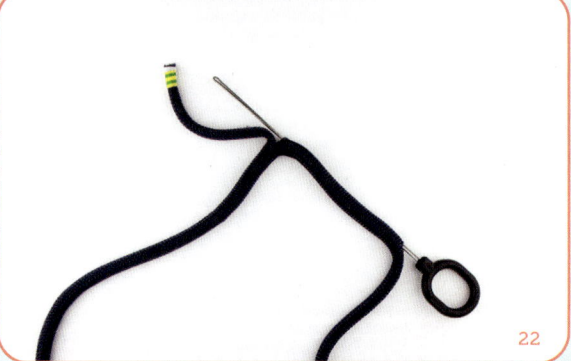

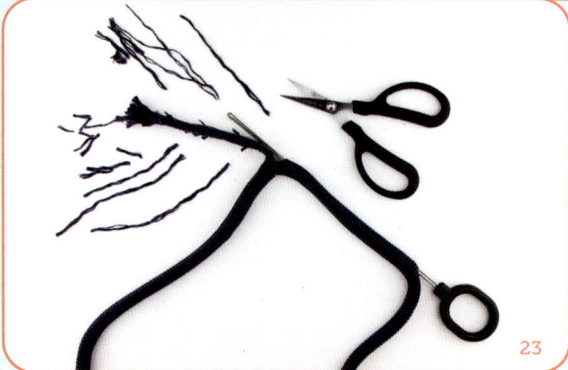

Taper the cover.

Pull through the tapered cover.

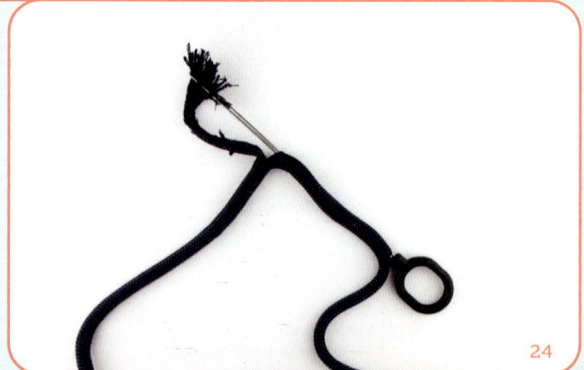

Milk the cover from the transition onwards.

Stitch the transition with whipping twine or make a stitched whipping.

This makes a continuous rope of double braid polyester, with extra strength.

# Single braid Dyneema ('loop')

Dyneema loops are light and strong and are therefore very suitable for attaching a block to the deck. In many cases they can also replace stainless steel D-shackles.

## Basic loop

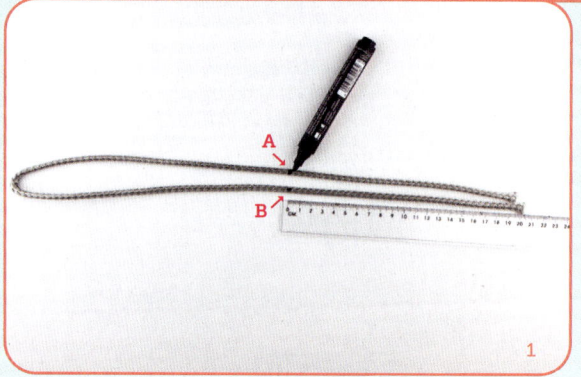

Double up the rope and mark two points (A and B) at a distance of 60 times the rope's diameter (18cm for a 3mm rope). The rope's total length should be around five times this (90cm for a 3mm rope).

Mark point M halfway on the rope.

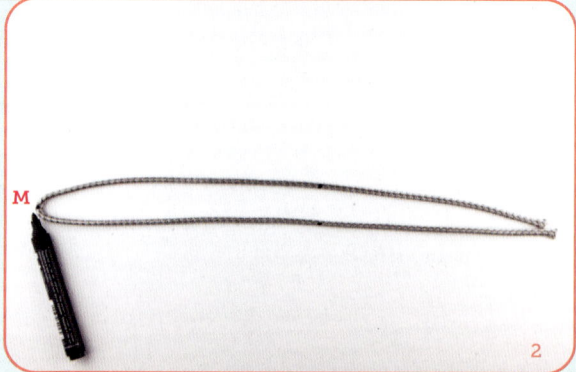

Insert a pulling needle into point M and pull it out at point A.

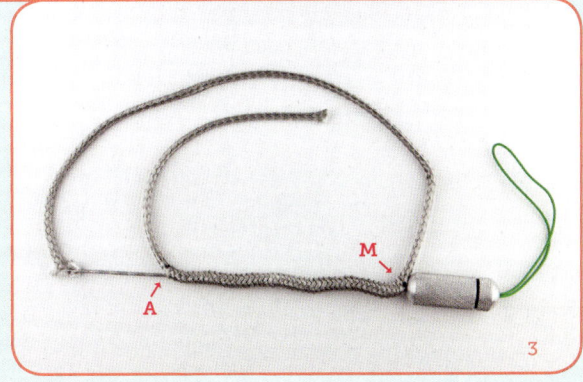

Tuck the rope back into itself and secure it with a needle as shown.

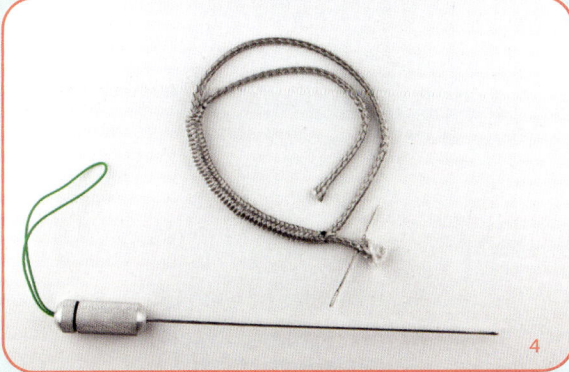

Insert the pulling needle into point M again and pull it out at point B. Pull the other, loose tail back out.

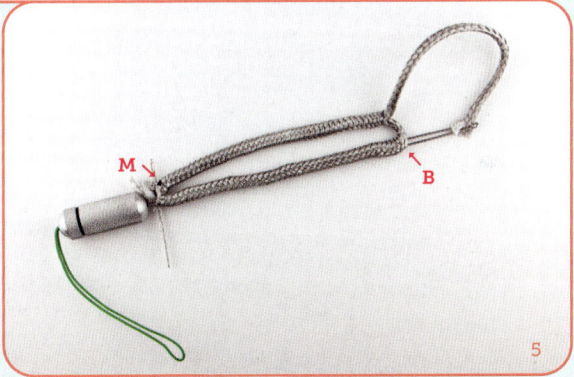

Taper both ends.

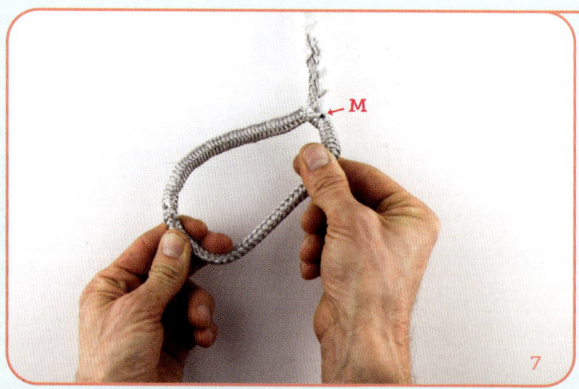

At point M, stretch out both sides of the loop.

Put some tension on the loop.

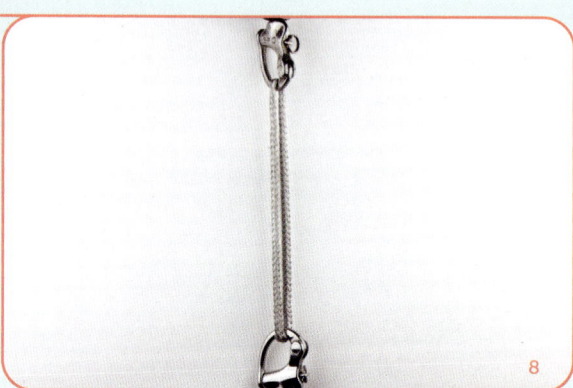

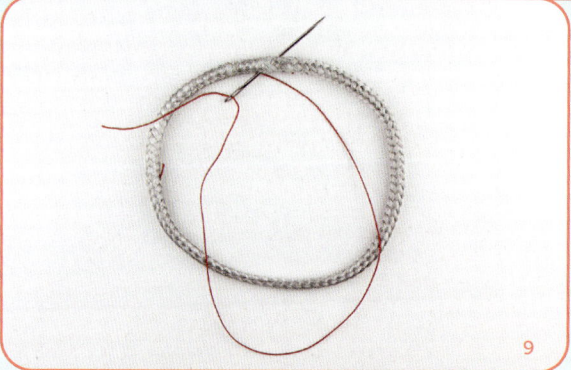

Secure the loop with some stitches.

This creates a basic Dyneema loop.

# Loop with cover

If you want a short and very strong Dyneema loop, you can multiply the rope's breaking load by doubling up the line. This method allows you to decide on the strength and size of your loop. In the example below the line has been looped four times, which multiplies the breaking load by about eight. Given that the rope's breaking load is 500kg, it would in theory be increased to 4,000kg. Use this type of loop where the loop has to be short and you know it has to endure very strong forces.

You'll need single braid Dyneema rope and a (Dyneema) cover to make this loop.

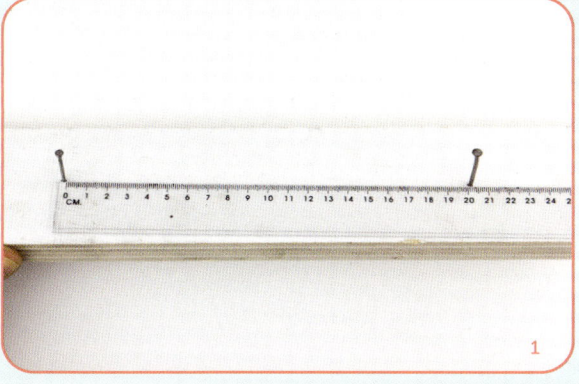

Determine the size of the loop and fix two nails on a wooden board to mark that length.

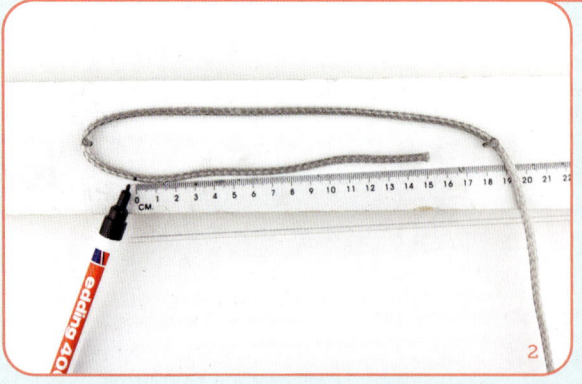

Mark the rope at 60 times the rope diameter (18cm for a 3mm rope).

Loop the rope around the nails as many times as needed to achieve your desired strength. Here it has been looped four times. Mark the rope where it meets the original mark made in step 2.

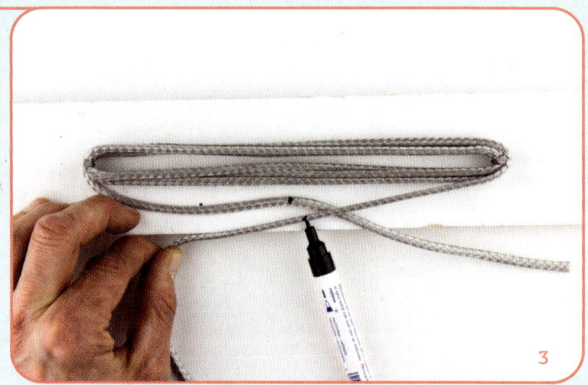

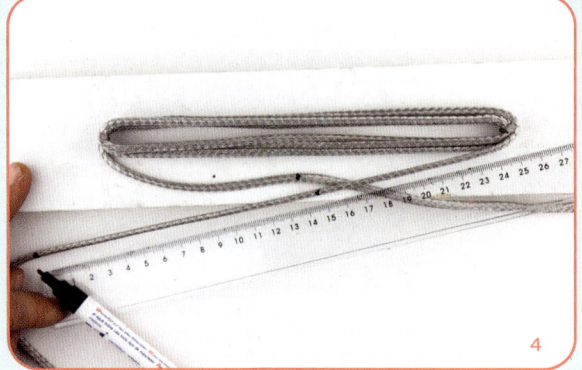

Measure 60 times the rope diameter again and cut the rope at that point (18cm for a 3mm rope).

Take a Dyneema cover at least three times the length of the loop (20 × 3mm = 60cm in this example).

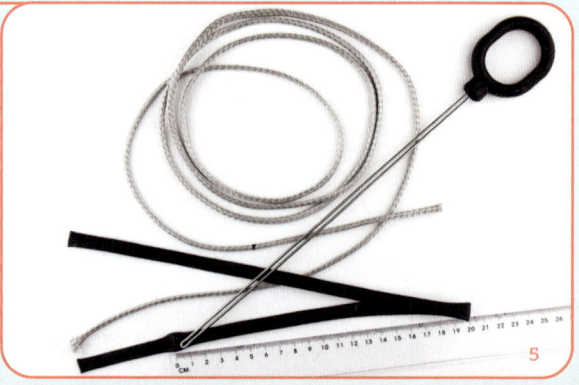

Insert a pulling needle into the cover about 10cm from the end and pull the cover around the needle.

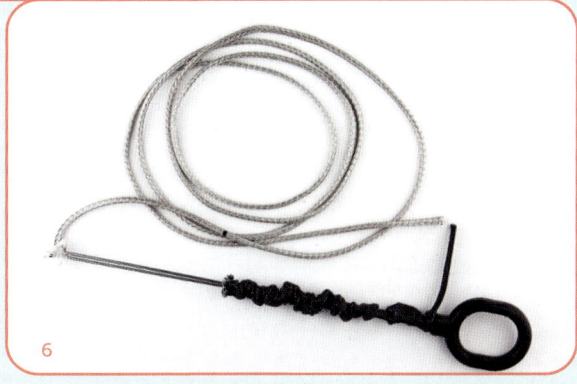

6

Pull the rope through the cover.

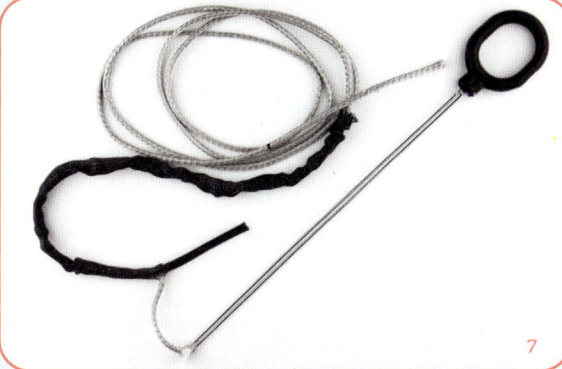

7

Insert the pulling needle into the cover again and repeat the steps above.

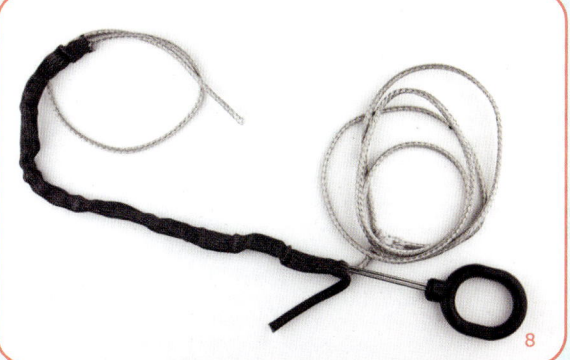

8

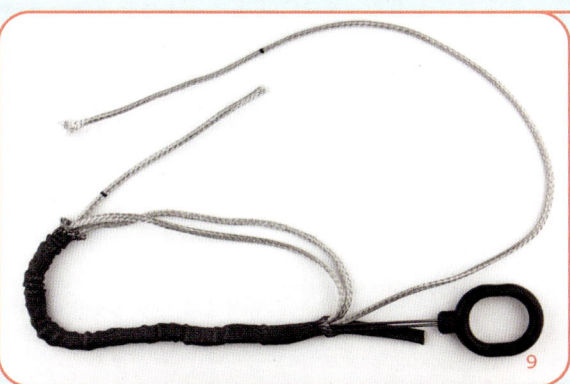

9

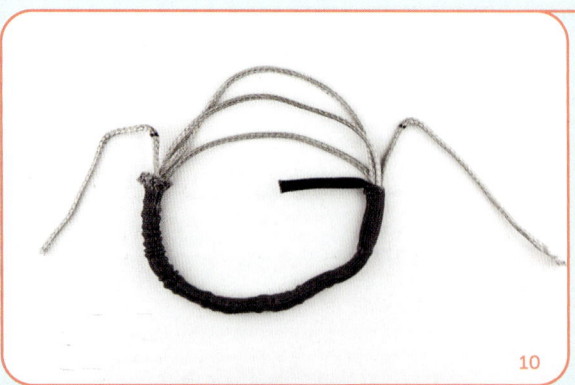

10

Pull out the tails from the cover. Insert a pulling needle in at such distance from the mark that the other tail can be completely buried inside.

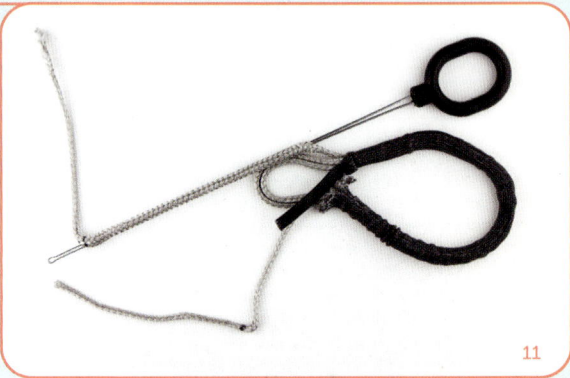

11

12

Secure the tail with a needle at a point where it emerges.

Pull the other tail through the rope as well.

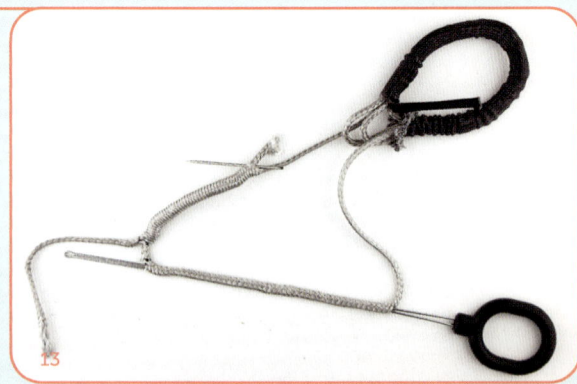

13

156

Taper both ends.

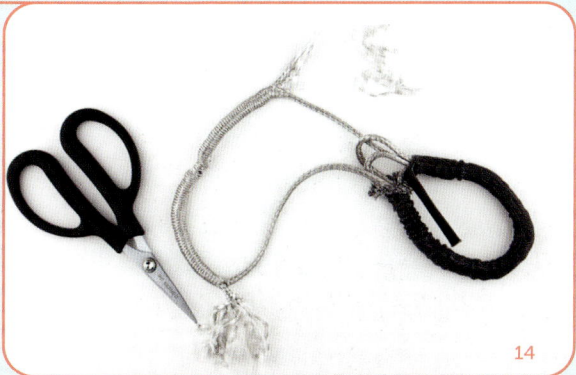

14

Milk the rope from the centre at both sides.

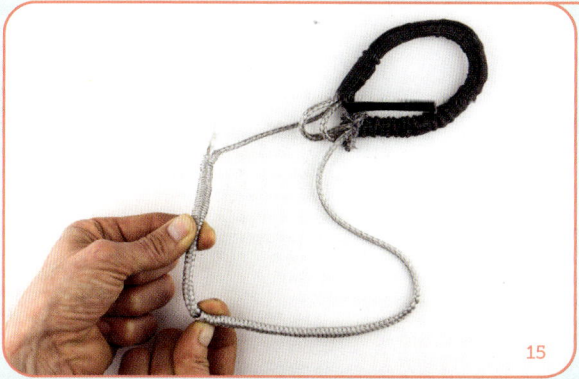

15

Secure the transitions with a few stitches to prevent them from slipping when they're not subject to any tension.

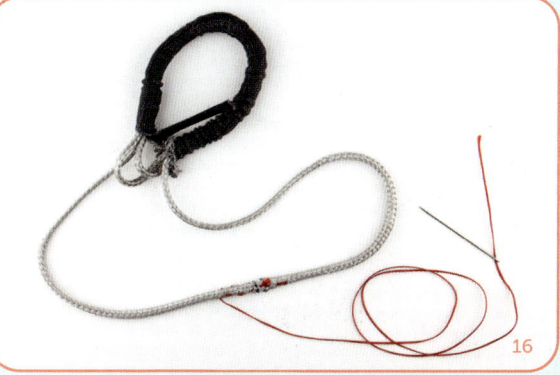

16

Shape the loop and tightly tape the cover to the ropes.

17

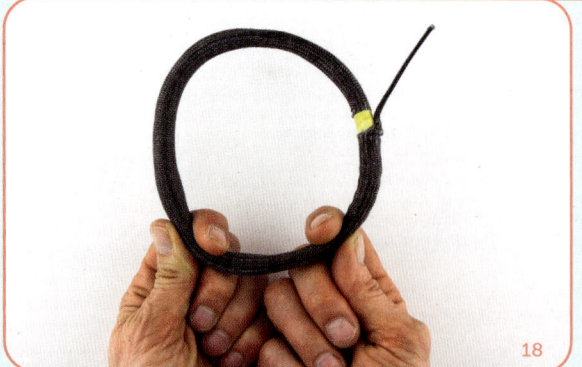

Put the loose tail of the cover over the tape.

18

Tuck the tail of the cover back in and secure the cover with a whipping.

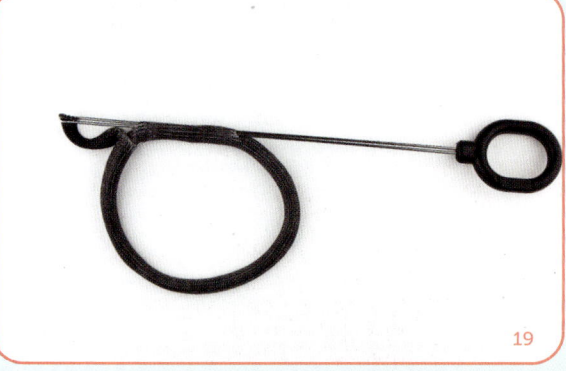

19

This results in a Dyneema loop with cover.

20

# Double braid Dyneema

The core provides the full strength of a double braid Dyneema rope. This splice is largely similar to the one on page 142, except that the Dyneema core is taken back into itself over a larger distance.

Tie two knots at about 2 metres. Create some space in the rope by cutting out at least 10–15cm of the core from the end.

Keep the core and cover together at the tail end and tuck up the spare cover towards the knot. Repeat on the other tail.

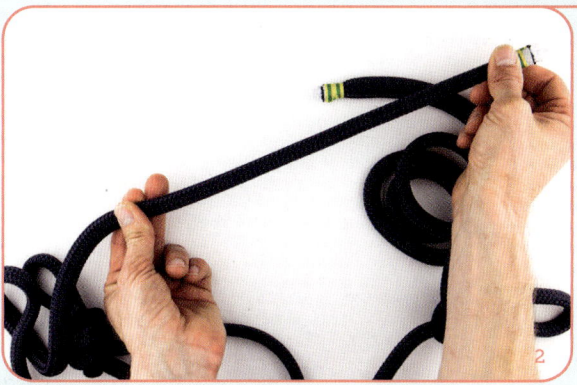

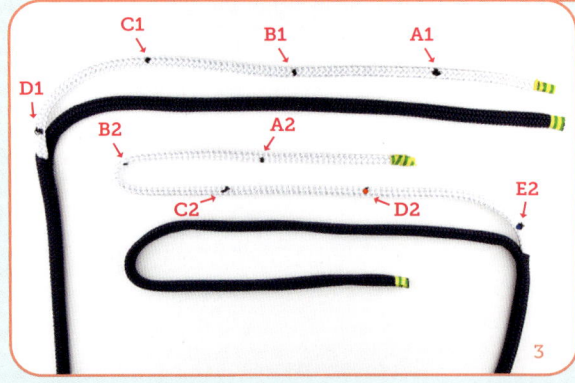

Rope 1: Pull out the core from the cover at four times the fid length and mark each fid length (A1, B1, C1, D1).

Rope 2: Repeat, but with five times the fid length instead (mark A2, B2, C2, D2, E2.

Insert the fid into the cover of rope 1 at one fid length and pull through the core of rope 2.

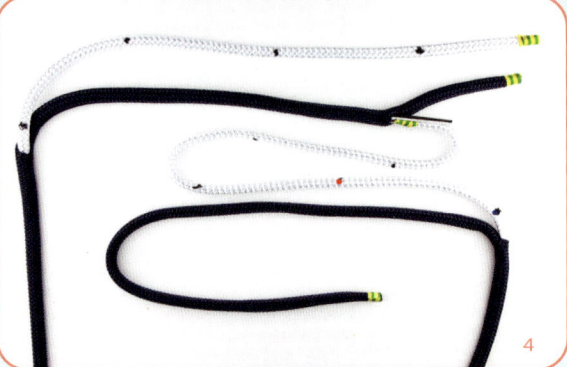

Pull the fid out of the cove at the point where the core of rope 1 emerges.

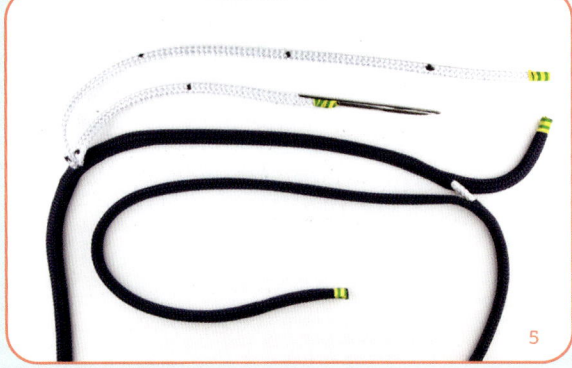

Cut the other core (rope 1, which hasn't passed through the cover) at twice the fid length from the tail end.

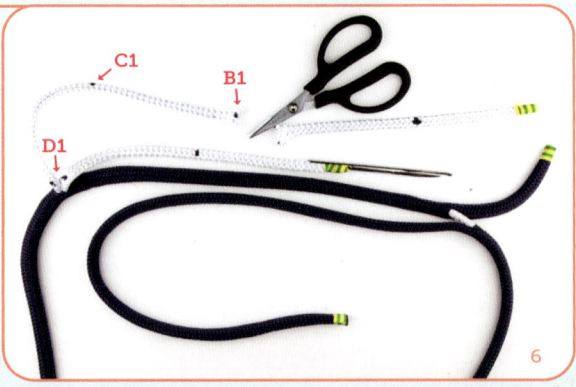

Take the uncut core (rope 2) into
the core at D1.

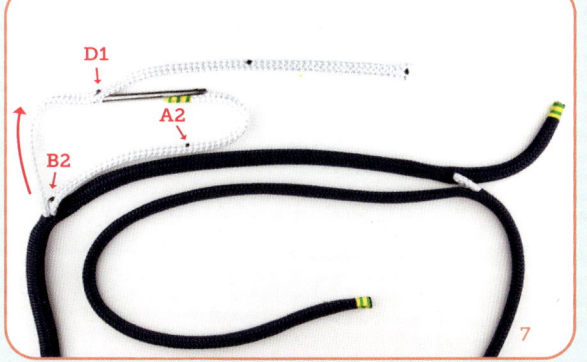

Pull out the fid at such a distance
that the core can be completely
buried inside up to point B2
(two fid length).

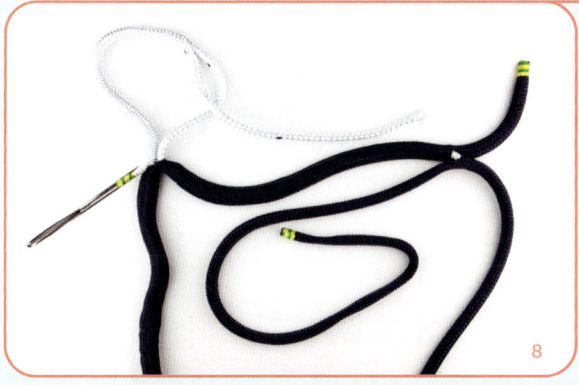

Secure a tail of the uncut core (rope
2) with a needle. Insert fid into the
core at point B2.

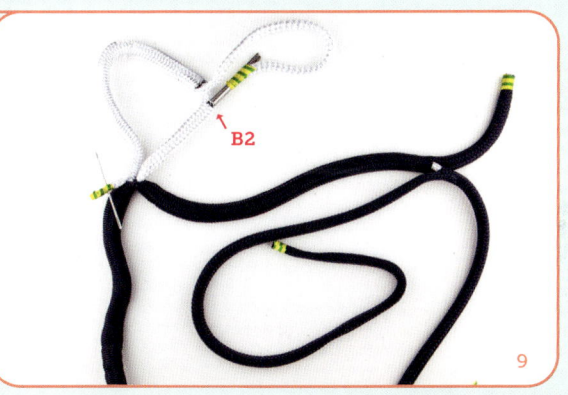

Again, pull out the fid at such a
distance that one core can be
completely buried inside the other.

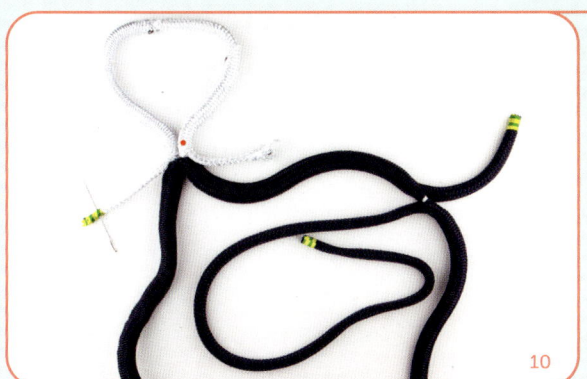

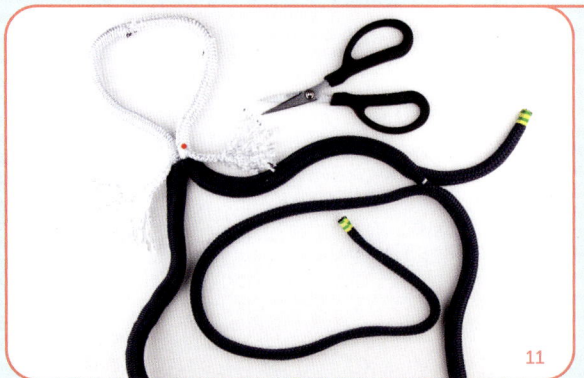

Taper the core at both ends.
Continue with steps 13–26 on
pages 146–149.

This creates a continuous rope from
double braid Dyneema.

163

# 12 Whippings

A whipping prevents the end of a rope from fraying. In double braid ropes it ensures that the core and cover are kept together. You'll need whipping twine, a strong needle and usually a palm. The width of the whipping should be approximately one to one and a half times the rope's diameter.

## Stitched whipping for braided ropes

Ropes with a braided core will always need a stitched whipping; a common whipping will slide off too easily. It will also prevent the core from slipping into the cover.

A stitched whipping is also used to finish an eye splice.

Sew the whipping twine to the rope with several stitches.

1

Wrap the twine around the stitches tightly.

Make sure the whipping is about one to one-and-a-half times as wide as the rope diameter (10–15mm for a 10mm rope).

Feed the needle straight through the rope right after the final whip.

Secure the whipping with two loops perpendicular to it.

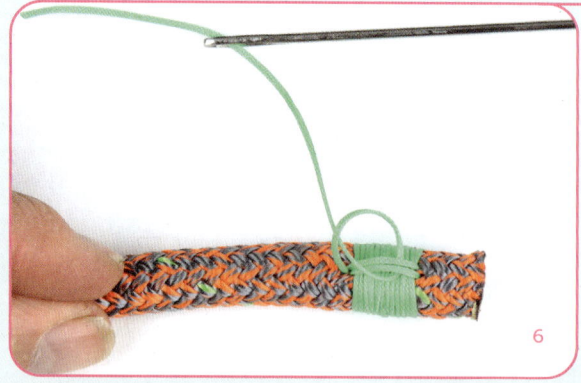

Finish with a half hitch around the loop.

6

Feed the needle through the other end of the rope.

7

8

Tie a half hitch around the loop this side, too. Work the twine back through the rope and cut it.

This creates a stitched whipping for braided ropes.

9

# Common whipping

This is the easiest whipping, but it has some disadvantages: it will slip off the rope quickly and it can easily break. It will also fall off if the whipping twine wears through at just one point.

Make a loop on top of the rope and wrap the twine tightly around it.

1

Work towards the tail end of the rope.

2

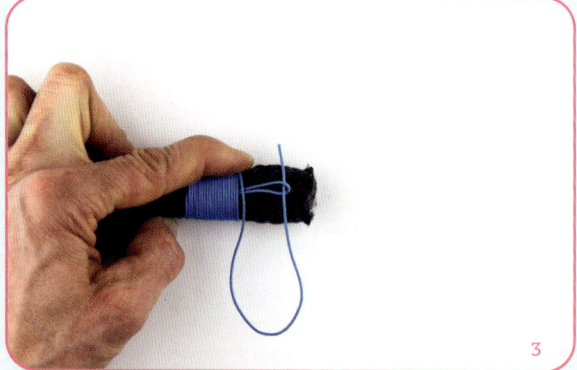

Make sure the whipping is about one and a half times as wide as the diameter of the rope (1.5cm for a 10mm rope). Feed the end of the twine through the loop.

Tightly pull the end of the loop under the whipping.

Cut the end of the twine. Pull on the end of the loop again. Cut and stow it back under the whipping with your scissors.

This creates a common whipping

# Whipping for a three-strand laid rope

This traditional method is not just very practical, it also looks great. This is the only whipping that will sit tightly on a three-strand laid rope.

Sew the whipping twine to the rope with several stitches.

Tightly wrap the twine around the stitches. Make sure the whipping is about one and a half times as wide as the rope's diameter (1.5cm for a 10mm rope).

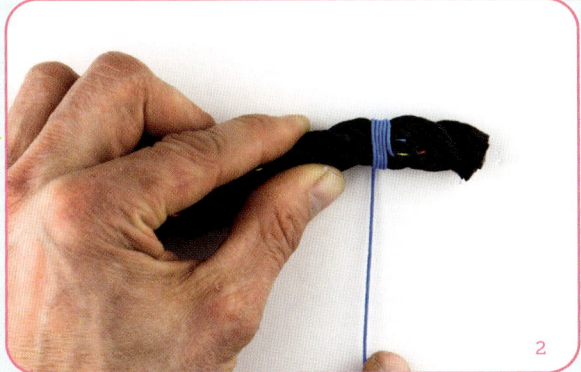

After the final whip, take the needle and insert it below one of the strands.

Put one stitch around the whipping and take it below the next strand. Turn the rope.

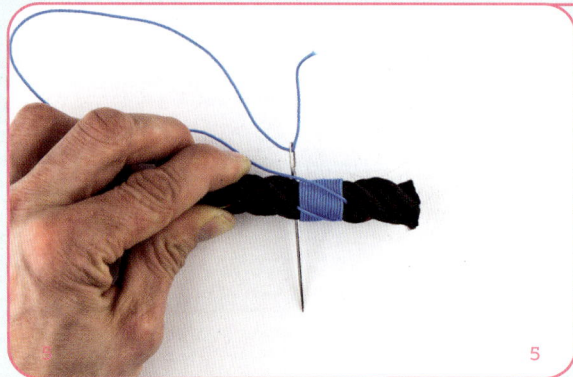

Make a loop around each strand.

Repeat this process until you have two loops stitched around each strand.

Finish with a half hitch and work it through to the next strand.

Tie another half hitch, take it through to the next strand and cut the twine.

This creates whipping on a three-strand laid rope.

# 13 Reeving of new halyards

There are several ways to reeve your newly bought halyards. If you are using a mouse line, make a reeving eye (see below) or a reeving loop (see page 174). If your old halyard is still in the mast, stitch it to the new halyard as shown in the photo below.

Sew the old halyard to the new one. You could wrap the join tightly with tape to make passage through the mast easier.

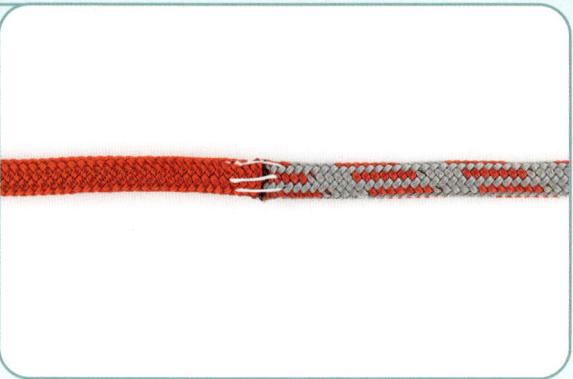

## Reeving eye ('Flemish eye')

A reeving eye or 'Flemish eye' is made up of only the rope's cover. There won't be any thickening in the rope because the core is removed. Bear in mind that this is not a very strong eye; it is merely used to feed a rope through the mast.

Pull out about 60cm of core from the cover and cut it.

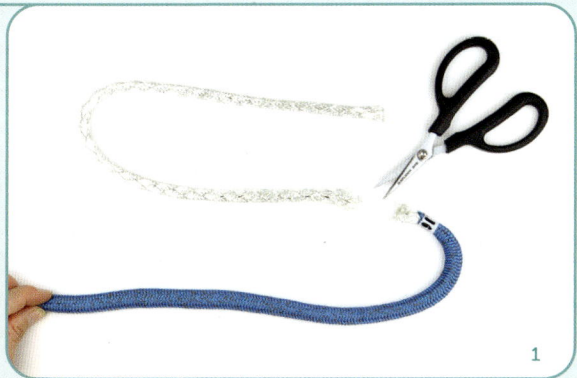

1

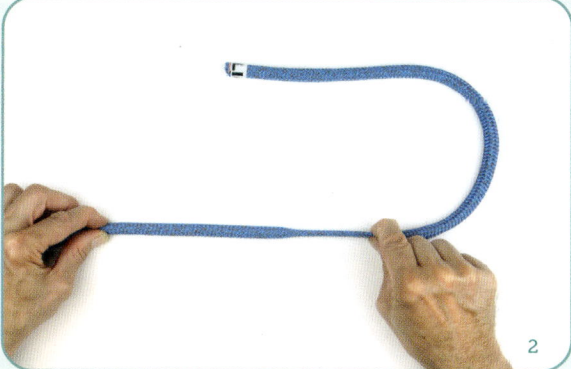

2

Stretch the cover so it is not riding up at any point.

Insert a pulling needle where the core ends and pull it 20–25 cm further out.

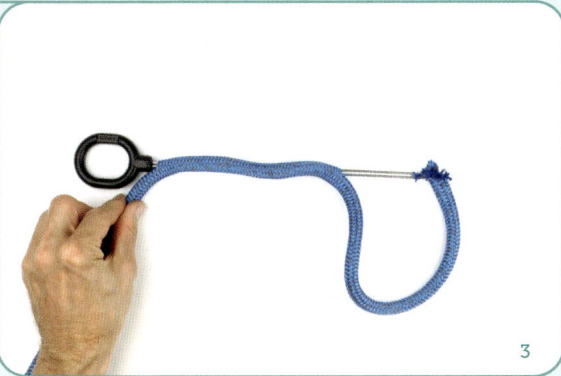

3

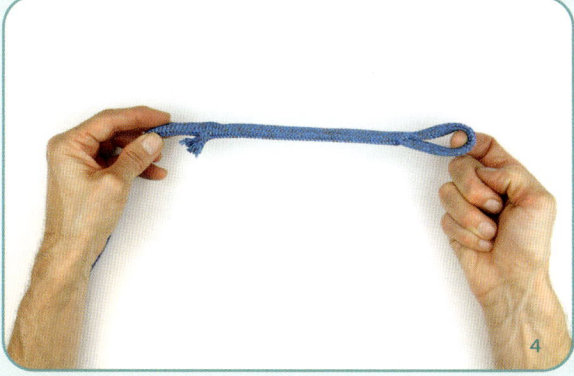

4

Tuck the cover back into itself. Pull the eye to make the core disappear into itself.

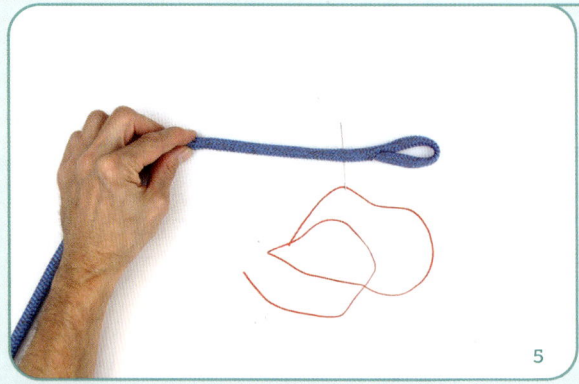

Add a stitched whipping (page 164) to fix the eye.

5

This creates a reeving eye.

6

# Reeving loop with whipping

In the photos below, you can see a stitched whipping with a fixed loop. You'll be able to kill two birds with one stone: the rope will have a smooth finish and you'll have a permanent loop that allows you to take the halyard out of the mast with a mouse line.

Use whipping twine to sew a big enough loop for your purposes to the end of the rope and continue it as a stitched whipping (see page 164).

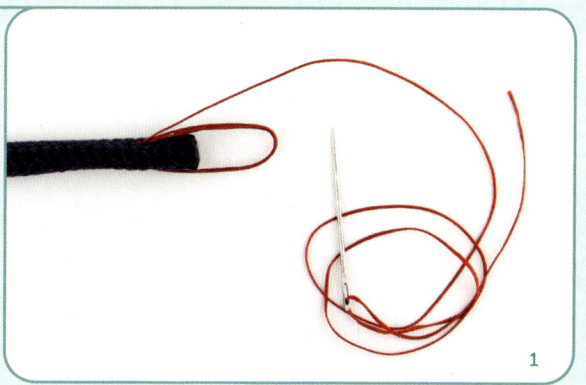

This creates a reeving loop with whipping.

# 14  Splicing tools

In some situations there is not much room to feed through a fid. Soft fids may prove to be the solution. You can easily make one from a Dyneema cover and a single braid Dyneema rope. Make sure you use a Dyneema cover because they are smooth and thin. Feed the rope you want to pull through in the Dyneema cover. This cover will become tight around the rope once you try to pull it. Once the soft fid is eased out you can slide the cover off.

## Using a soft fid

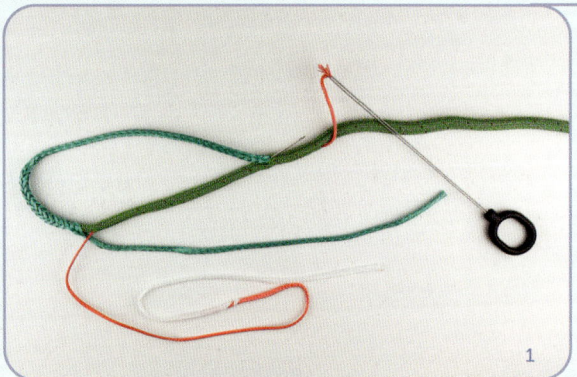

Use a pulling needle to feed the soft fid through the rope.

Insert the core into the cover of the soft fid.

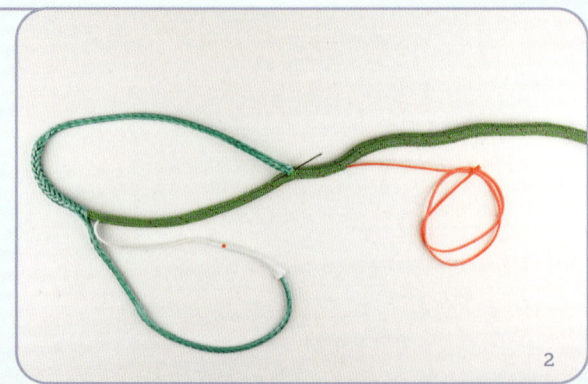

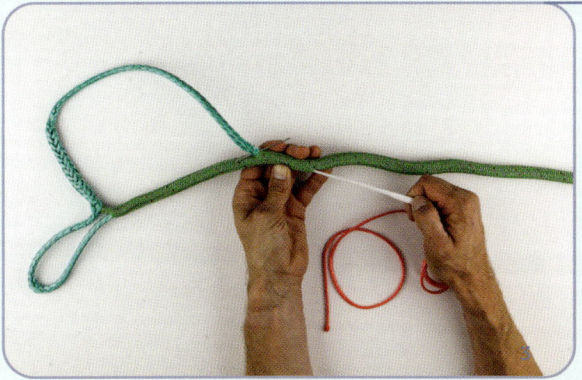

Pull the core through the rope cover with the soft fid.

## How to make a soft fid

A soft fid comprises two ropes: a thin Dyneema rope to grip, and a Dyneema cover that holds the rope to be pulled through. Join the two ropes with a lock splice

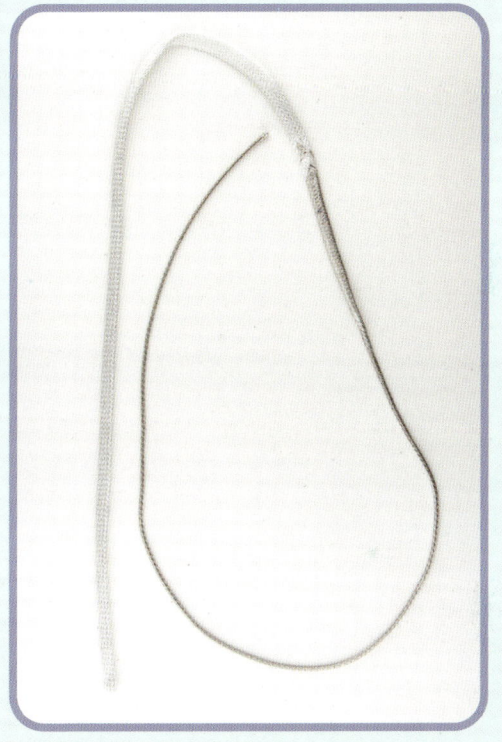

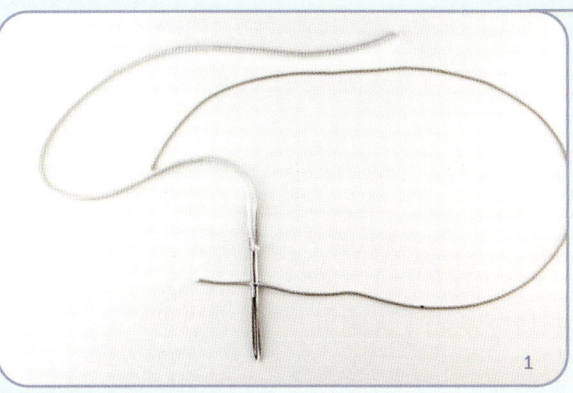

Take a Dyneema cover of around 50cm length and a single braid Dyneema rope of at least one metre length and a diameter of 3–4mm. Insert a fid about 5cm along from the end of the rope and pull through the cover.

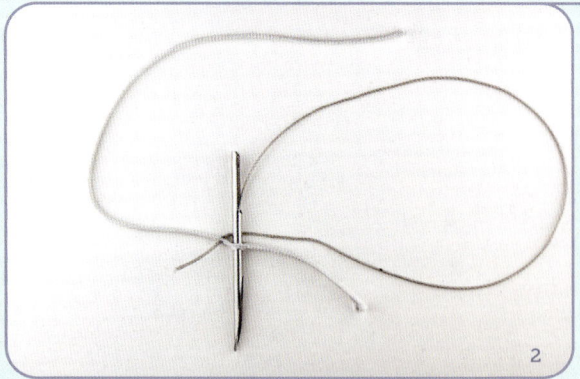

Insert the fid through the cover, just next to the junction from step 1, and pull through the rope.

The lock is in place.

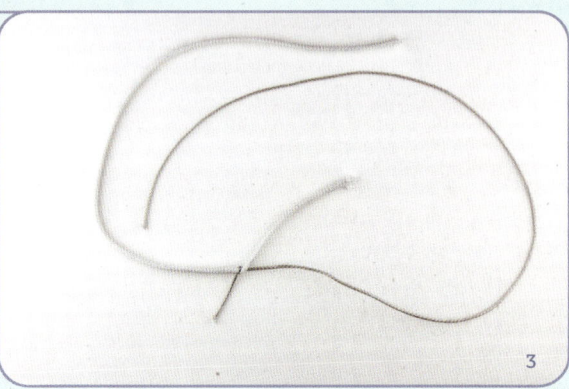

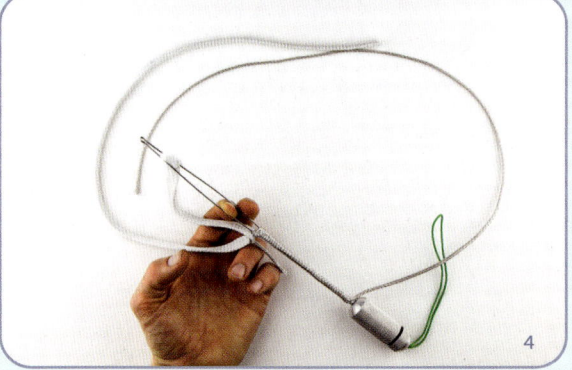

Insert a pulling needle into the rope and pull the cover back out.

Taper the cover by cutting it diagonally.

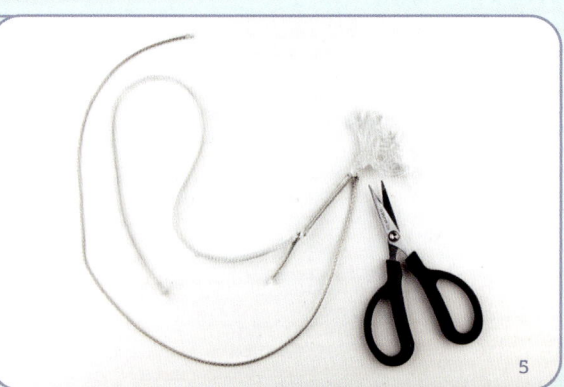

Pull the end of the rope through the cover.

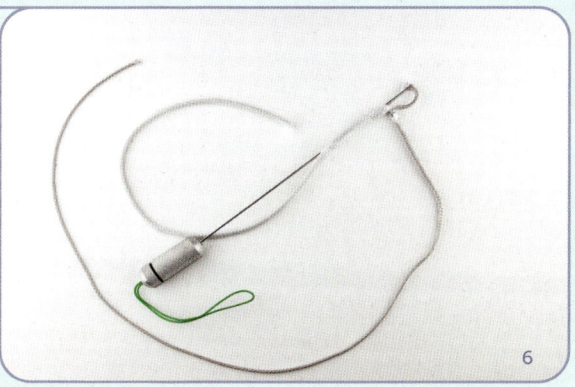

Milk the rope and the cover back from the centre.

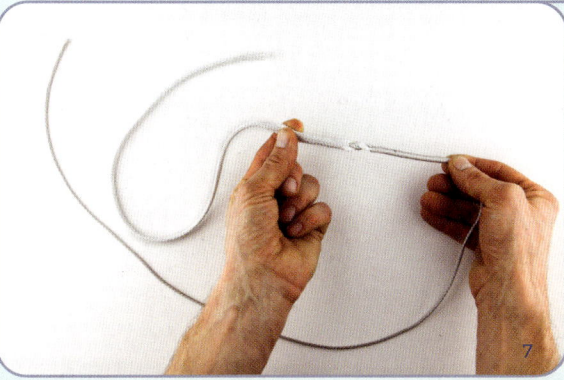

This creates a soft fid.

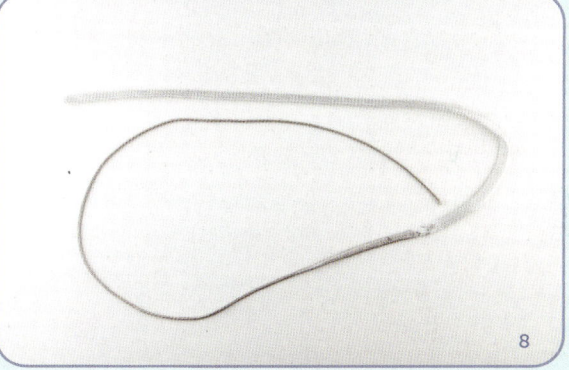

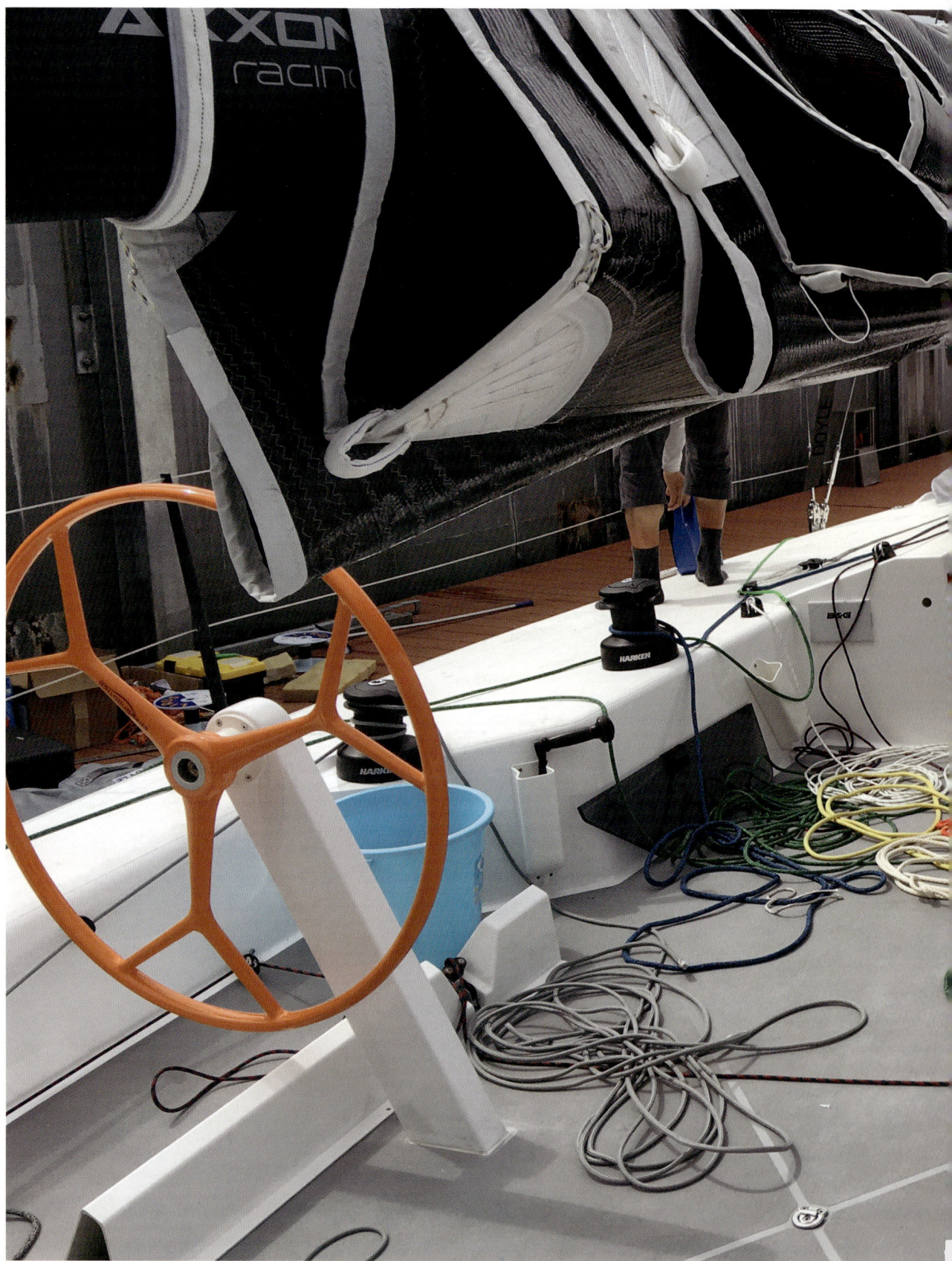

# 1. Features of synthetic fibres: a comparison

Below you will find a comparison table to assess the main features of synthetic fibres. Every material differs, depending on the quality of the material, its treatment and the construction of the rope. More information about the fibres can be found in Chapter 1.

| Material | Common brand names | Stretch at breaking | Indicative break load (ф 8mm [kg])* | Density [kg/dm³] | Melting point [°C] | UV resistance (1 = low 5 = high) | Durability (1 = low 5 = high) | Loss of strength at knots (%) | Main use |
|---|---|---|---|---|---|---|---|---|---|
| Polypropylene (PP) | | 30% | 1,000 | 0.91 (floating) | 170 | 2 | 2 | 35–45% | Mooring line/ tow line |
| HMPE (Ultra High Molecular Weight Polyethylene) | Dyneema, Spectra, Stirotex | 3.5% | 5,000 | 0.97 (floating) | 145 | 5 | 5 | 50–65% | Halyard/sheet/ trimming line |
| Polybenzobisoxazole (PBO) | Zylon | 2.5% | 8,000 | 1.56 | 650 ** | 1 | 2 | 45–65% | **Standing rigging/cover (Regatta)** |
| Liquid Crystal Polymer | Vectran | 3.3% | 4,500 | 1.41 | 330 | 2 | 3 | 65–70% | Halyard/ rigging |
| Polyester (PES) | Dacron, Diolen | 15% | 1,800 | 1.38 | 260 | 5 | 5 | 40–45% | Halyard/sheet/ control line |
| Polyamide (PA) | Nylon | 20% | 1,350 | 1.14 | 220–250 | 4 | 4 | 35–40% | Mooring line/ anchor rode |
| Aramid | Kevlar, Technora | 3% to 4% | 4,600 | 1.39 | 500 | 2 | 3 | 60–70% | Sheet covers (regatta) |

* The given breakload is an indication and can vary between manufacturers due to construction methods.

** No melting point but point of degradation.

## What elongation do ropes have on board?

Elongation, often called stretch, is a very important parameter for ropes. On the one hand, for mooring lines we want quite a bit of elongation in a rope, as they need to be able to absorb the shocks caused by wind and waves. On the other hand, for halyards, sheets and trimlines, we should choose ropes with as little elongation as possible.

## Elongation is dependent on the applied load

The amount of elongation depends on the amount of load that is applied. The fibre properties give a good indication of how much elongation we will see in practice. Typically, elongation of fibre properties are stated at break. By taking the ratio between applied load divided by break load and multiply this with the elongation at break you have a good indication of the expected elongation for a fibre.

Most applications use a safe working load (SWL) of 20% of the break load (= safety factor 5). So the expected maximum amount of elongation for a fibre will be:

$20/100 \times$ fibre elongation at break

A polyester fibre at break has an elongation of 15%. At 20% of the break load, the elongation will only be around $20/100 \times 15\% = 3\%$. The table below shows this analysis for all commonly used fibres for ropes.

| Fibre | PBO | Aramid | SK99 | Vectran | SK78 | HMPE | DM20 | Technora | SK38 | Polyester | PA | PP |
|---|---|---|---|---|---|---|---|---|---|---|---|---|
| Elongation at break | 2.5% | 3% | 3.2% | 3.3% | 3.5% | 3.5% | 3.6% | 4% | 7.5% | 15% | 20% | 30% |
| Elongation at SWL (= 20% of the BL) | 0.5% | 0.6% | 0.6% | 0.7% | 0.7% | 0.7% | 0.7% | 0.8% | 1.5% | 3.0% | 4.0% | 6.0% |

On a boat, ropes will normally not exceed a load of 20% of the break load of polyester. Polyester is often the reference material. Example: a standard diameter of a halyard for a 34ft boat is typically 10mm. The load on this halyard will not exceed 20% of the break load of a 10mm polyester rope. So, in order to get a good indication of the actual elongation of a halyard on board we should look at the load of 20% of the break load of polyester.

In the graph below we combined the fibre strength, also a fibre property, with the elongation. The fibre strength is indexed with polyester being 100. A straight line was drawn between elongation at break with a corresponding index to 0.

| Fibre | PBO | Aramid | SK99 | Vectran | SK78 | HMPE | DM20 | Technora | SK38 | Polyester | PA | PP |
|---|---|---|---|---|---|---|---|---|---|---|---|---|
| Elongation at break | 2.5% | 3% | 3.2% | 3.3% | 3.5% | 3.5% | 3.6% | 4% | 7.5% | 15% | 20% | 30% |
| Strength index (PES=100) | 450 | 255 | 328 | 250 | 273 | 234 | 242 | 269 | 129 | 100 | 73 | 51 |

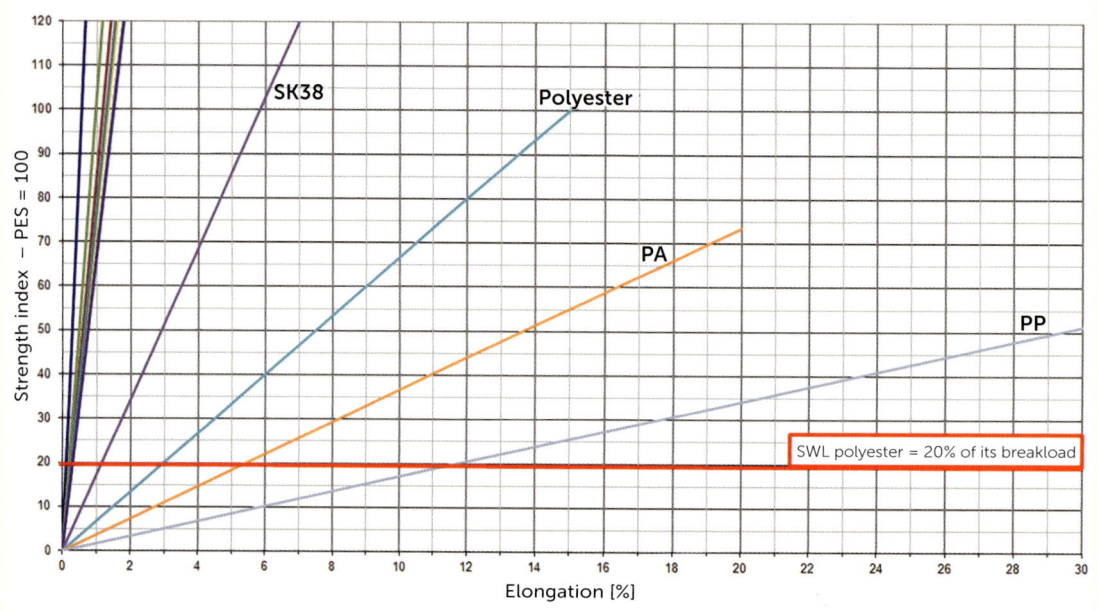

Fibre Strength index versus Elongation

Following the red horizontal line, the SWL of polyester, you can draw some interesting conclusions:

- If you replace a polyester halyard with a Dyneema SK78 halyard of the same diameter, the elongation will reduce from about 3% to only 0.3%. For a 15m halyard this means for polyester 45cm and for Dyneema SK78 only 4.5cm elongation.

- There is no significant difference in elongation between most of the high-performance fibres: PBO/ARAMID/Dyneema SK99/VECTRAN/SK78/HMPE/DM20/Technora. You will not notice a large difference in performance between using any of these materials for your halyard.

- Dyneema SK38 (and other poorer quality HMPE not shown in this graph) is an exception and has an elongation of around 1.2%. A rope with this fibre is not suitable for a regatta sailor using laminated sails as the elongation is too large.

This theoretical analysis based on fibre properties was carried out by Klaus Hemmers from Teufelberger. Thereafter, the data was tested in practice. After preloading the test ropes at 40–50% of the break load, they confirmed the elongation of the theoretical graph. Preloading is required to take out all initial braiding elongation. It is important to realise that new ropes without preloading will initially show more elongation.

# 2. Diameters and breaking loads of ropes

## Calculating breaking loads for sheets and halyards

We use Roger Marshall's formula to calculate the loads on sheets. This formula works for the most common yachts. Loads can vary slightly for a catamaran or laminate sails. The following components are needed to use the Marshall formula:

(A) = surface area of the sail in m$^2$

(V) = wind speed in knots

The formula results in the sheet load in kg.

**Sheet Load (headsail sheet) = (A) × (V)$^2$ × 0.021**

If you want to know the breaking loads of your ropes, multiply the outcome of the formula by five, to incorporate a safety factor.

The formula reflects nicely the square relationship of the wind with the load on a rope, unlike the surface area of the sail. So while a storm sail may be smaller, it requires thicker ropes because you use this sail at higher wind speeds.

Two other factors need to be taken into account: where the boom is attached and the purchase on the sheet. The Marshall formula assumes that the mainsheet is attached at the far end of the boom. However, if it is attached somewhere halfway along, the load on the mainsheet would double. I have incorporated this leverage effect and adapted the Marshall formula for mainsheets.

(X) = The distance (m) from the boom end to the point where the mainsheet is attached

(E) = Boom length (m)

**Sheet load (mainsheet) = (A) × (V)$^2$ × 0.021 × ((E)/(E−X))**

If the purchase on the mainsheet is four, the load on the mainsheet is divided by four. The forces on the mainsheet travellers will stay the same.

The tensile strengths for halyards are generally similar to the loads on the sheets. Hence you can use the same formula as the one for the headsail sheets. The forces can vary by up to about 20%, depending on the rigging. This is negligible when you use a safety factor of five.

## Guidelines for the diameters of sheets and halyards

You can find the guidelines for the diameter of sheets and halyards with a polyester core in the table below. If you choose a core made of high-performance fibres, such as Dyneema, you can generally use a rope that is 2mm thinner.

| Boat length | Sheets* | | | Halyards* | | |
|---|---|---|---|---|---|---|
| | Main | Genoa | Spinnaker | Main | Genoa | Spinnaker |
| 6–8 metres | 10 mm | 10 mm | 10 mm | 8 mm | 8 mm | 8 mm |
| 9 metres | 10 mm | 12 mm | 10 mm | 10 mm | 10 mm | 8 mm |
| 10 metres | 12 mm | 14 mm | 10 mm | 10 mm | 10 mm | 10 mm |
| 11 metres | 12 mm | 14 mm | 12 mm | 10 mm | 12 mm | 10 mm |
| 12 metres | 12 mm | 14 mm | 12 mm | 12 mm | 12 mm | 12 mm |
| 14 metres | 14 mm | 14 mm | 14 mm | 12 mm | 12 mm | 12 mm |
| 16 metres | 14 mm | 14 mm | 14 mm | 12 mm | 14 mm | 12 mm |
| 18 metres | 14 mm | 14 mm | 14 mm | 14 mm | 14 mm | 14 mm |

## Guidelines for the diameters of mooring lines

The table below shows the guidelines for the diameters of polyester or polyamide mooring lines. Note that polypropylene (PPM) is weaker and thus needs to be about 2–4mm thicker than the diameters given in the table.

The boat length is usually a good reference for the diameter of mooring lines and anchor rode. In the right column of the table you'll find the weight of the boat.

| Boat length | Polyester and polyamide mooring lines** | Approximate boat weight*** |
|---|---|---|
| 8 metres | 10 mm | 1–2 tons |
| 10 metres | 12 mm | 4 tons |
| 12 metres | 14 mm | 6.5 tons |
| 14 metres | 16 mm | 11 tons |
| 16 metres | 18 mm | 12 tons |
| 20 metres | 20 mm | 16 tons |
| 28 metres | 24 mm | 20 tons |

\* Source: Seilflechter Tauwerk

\*\* Source: Gleistein Ropes

\*\*\* Source: Marlow Ropes

# Acknowledgements

Quite a few people have supported me and advised me while I was producing this book.

I'd like to thank in particular: António Lima, Ben Rutte, Deirdre Polman, Diogo Cayolla, Dominic Bakker, Eugenio Follender Grossfeld, Jac Spijkers, Marc Thiry, Massimo Dell'Acqua, Klaus Hemmers, and Simen Polman.

I would be happy to receive suggestions and feedback via info@splicingropes.com

# About the author

Jan-Willem Polman is a sailor, entrepreneur and mechanical engineer who specialises in synthetics technology. From 2008 to 2010 he sailed around the world with his wife and two young children. After that, he gave up corporate life and devoted himself to being an entrepreneur. He is currently the head of several watersports companies that specialise in ropes. He organises workshops and courses about splicing modern ropes. He also developed the D-Splicer needles that are used widely by sailors and riggers.

www.splicingropes.com

# Bibliography

Danilo Fabbroni, *Rigging*. Chichester: John Wiley & Sons; 2008.

Gleistein Ropes, *Splicebook*. Bremen: Gleistein Ropes; 2010.

Barbara Merry & John Darwin, *The Splicing Handbook*. London: Adlard Coles; 2011.

Gordon Perry & Steve Judkins, *Knots, Splices & Ropework*. Hamble: Royal Yachting Association; 2008

# Index